SPORT AND PERFORMANCE IN THE TWENTY-FIRST CENTURY

Analyzing sport through the lens of performance and theorizing performance through the lens of sport, *Sport and Performance in the Twenty-First Century* offers a field intervention, a series of in-depth performance analyses, and an investigation of the intersection between sport performances and public life in the historical present.

The objectives of this book are three-fold. First, the book advocates for the study of sport in the fields of Theatre and Performance Studies and, through in-depth performance analyses, demonstrates how the critical language and methods of performance studies help illuminate the manifold impacts of the practices, activities, and events of sport. Second, the book introduces new critical language that was originally developed in conjunction with sport but is also designed for cross-genre performance analysis. In introducing novel terminology, the book aims to simultaneously facilitate analysis of sport performances and to demonstrate how the study of sport can contribute to the fields of Theatre and Performance Studies. Finally, the book investigates the epistemological, affective, and socio-political effects of sport performances in order to illuminate how sport performances influence, and are influenced by, their historical conditions.

This study will be of great interest to students and scholars in Theatre and Performance Studies, Physical Culture Studies, and Socio-Cultural Sports Studies.

Kelsey Blair is an Assistant Professor in the Department of English at Concordia University in Montreal. She is a theatre, performance, and cultural studies scholar, a university teacher, an author, and a freelance writer.

Routledge Advances in Theatre & Performance Studies

This series is our home for cutting-edge, upper-level scholarly studies and edited collections. Considering theatre and performance alongside topics such as religion, politics, gender, race, ecology, and the avant-garde, titles are characterized by dynamic interventions into established subjects and innovative studies on emerging topics.

Entangled Performance Histories
New Approaches to Theater Historiography
Erika Fischer-Lichte, Małgorzata Sugiera, Torsten Jost and Holger Hartung with Omid Soltani

Rechoreographing Learning
Dance As a Way to Bridge the Mind-Body Divide in Education
Sandra Cerny Minton

Politics as Public Art
The Aesthetics of Political Organizing and Social Movements
Martin Zebracki and Zane McNeill

Lessons for Today from Shakespeare's Classroom
The Learning Benefits of Drama and Rhetoric in Schools
Robin Lithgow

Notelets of Filth
An *Emilia* Companion Reader
Laura Kressly, Aida Patient, and Kimberly A. Williams

Transcultural Theater
Günther Heeg

For more information about this series, please visit: https://www.routledge.com/Routledge-Advances-in-Theatre--Performance-Studies/book-series/RATPS

SPORT AND PERFORMANCE IN THE TWENTY-FIRST CENTURY

Kelsey Blair

LONDON AND NEW YORK

Cover image: Kelsey Blair

First published 2023
by Routledge
4 Park Square, Milton Park, Abingdon, Oxon OX14 4RN

and by Routledge
605 Third Avenue, New York, NY 10158

Routledge is an imprint of the Taylor & Francis Group, an informa business

© 2023 Kelsey Blair

The right of Kelsey Blair to be identified as author of this work has been asserted in accordance with sections 77 and 78 of the Copyright, Designs and Patents Act 1988.

All rights reserved. No part of this book may be reprinted or reproduced or utilised in any form or by any electronic, mechanical, or other means, now known or hereafter invented, including photocopying and recording, or in any information storage or retrieval system, without permission in writing from the publishers.

Trademark notice: Product or corporate names may be trademarks or registered trademarks, and are used only for identification and explanation without intent to infringe.

British Library Cataloguing-in-Publication Data
A catalogue record for this book is available from the British Library

Library of Congress Cataloging-in-Publication Data
Names: Blair, Kelsey, author.
Title: Sport and performance in the twenty-first century / Kelsey Blair.
Other titles: Sport and performance in the 21st century
Description: First Edition. | New York : Routledge, 2023. |
Identifiers: LCCN 2022035198 (print) | LCCN 2022035199 (ebook) | ISBN 9781032231280 (Hardback) | ISBN 9781032231297 (Paperback) | ISBN 9781003275879 (eBook)
Subjects: LCSH: Sports. | Performance.
Classification: LCC GV706.8 .B56 2023 (print) | LCC GV706.8 (ebook) | DDC 790--dc23/eng/20220811
LC record available at https://lccn.loc.gov/2022035198
LC ebook record available at https://lccn.loc.gov/2022035199

ISBN: 9781032231280 (hbk)
ISBN: 9781032231297 (pbk)
ISBN: 9781003275879 (ebk)

DOI: 10.4324/9781003275879

Typeset in Bembo
by KnowledgeWorks Global Ltd.

For my parents, Jim Blair and Joan Blair

CONTENTS

Acknowledgements   *viii*

Introduction: Sport and the Field of Performance   1

1   Performance Genres, Sport, and Match-Fixing at the 2012 Olympics   18

2   Configurations and Formations: The Patterning of Behaviour in Performance Activities   43

3   The Patterning of Audience Behaviours and Hockey in Canada   65

4   Sequences of Action across Genres: Injury Mini-Dramas and American Football   90

5   Gestural Marks in Sport Performance, The Genealogy of the Butterfly, and the Refugee Olympic Team   110

Conclusion   *130*
Appendix 1   *137*
Index   *139*

ACKNOWLEDGEMENTS

Laying on a gymnasium floor at my first basketball camp, I tossed a ball into the air and watched the rust-coloured leather spin. Gravity took hold, and the ball began to tumble toward me. I extended my arms, allowing the ball and its gently ribbed texture to land in my palms. It was, quite simply, the most thrilling experience. Arguably, it was also when I started writing this book. Unknowingly, I kept writing this book through my childhood and my time as a competitive swimmer, through my multisport teens, and into my basketball-filled young-adulthood. I started *actually* writing this book roughly ten years ago and am thankful for all the people who have supported me throughout.

The intellectual energy for this project was developed and maintained throughout my graduate studies in Vancouver, British Columbia, at the University of British Columbia and Simon Fraser University. My MA supervisor, Kirsty Johnston, encouraged me to pursue the intersection between sport and performance, supported me intellectually and professionally, and was a consistent source of rigour, wit, and boundless compassion. My PhD supervisor, Peter Dickinson, was immensely helpful with his thoughtful intellectual engagements, humour, and unparalleled editing skills. During this time, I also met a cohort of collaborators, colleagues, and friends in Selena Couture, Julia Henderson, Claire Carolan, Sandra Chamberlain-Snider, and Katrina Dunn, all of whom supported ideas and research at various stages of development. I am also grateful to Jocelyn Pitsch, who enlivened my thinking through passionate conversation and keen editorial wisdom while also being an inspiring and caring friend. During this time, I was welcomed into a community of rigorous and kind Canadian theatre and performance studies scholars including Marlis Schweitzer, Keren Zaiontz, Karen Fricker, Peter Kuling, Laura Levin,

Kim Solga, and Susan Bennett—all of whom have supported the development of chapters through various conference activities. I am particularly thankful to Keren Zaiontz—whose editorial skills guided one of my first publications—Susan Bennett—whose commentary on my doctoral dissertation was invaluable for the trajectory of this project—Erin Hurley—who offered theoretical wisdom and professional guidance as my postdoctoral supervisor—and to Kim Solga—for sharing her blog, her mentorship, and her editorial prowess. Thank you also to sport and performance scholars Shannon Walsh, Eero Laine, and Broderick Chow for their conference curation and editorial work that supported the development of various sport and performance-related essays.

Additionally, I have been fortunate to be the recipient of infrastructural and institutional support. Throughout my PhD, I received financial support from the Department of English at Simon Fraser University. I was also a recipient of a Social Sciences and Humanities Research Council doctoral fellowship and later a Social Sciences and Humanities Research Council postdoctoral fellowship, both of which permitted me to complete the research for this book. I would also like to thank Taylor & Francis for allowing me to republish portions of two essays: copyright 2018, "The 2012 Olympic Badminton Scandal: Match-Fixing, Code of Conduct Documents, and Women's Sport" by Kelsey Blair, from *The International Journal of Sport History*, reproduced by permission of Taylor & Francis Group, LLC, a division of Informa plc.; and copyright 2020, "The politics of performing the butterfly stroke" by Kelsey Blair, from *Sporting Performances: Politics in Play* edited by Shannon Walsh, reproduced by permission of Taylor & Francis Group, LLC, a division of Informa plc.

Throughout the latter stages of this project, my intellectual, professional, and personal communities continued to expand. Scott Mealey, Kelsey Jacobson, Signy Lynch, and Jenny Salisbury, co-directors of the Centre for Spectatorship and Audience Research: you continually push me to explore methods and areas of thought and have also provided me with a professional anchor full of gentle venting and lots of laughter. Megan Johnson: you are an intellectual teammate, who has the sharpest of theoretical minds and the most compassionate of hearts. Andréanne Larouche: your curiosity, expansive support, laughter, and care have shaped the texture of the last few years, at once softening days and strengthening me.

Finally, thank you to my parents, Jim Blair and Joan Blair. You have read drafts, talked me through ideas, laughed with me, laughed at me, and most importantly, reminded me that love is an action: when it is performed with the compassion, generosity, and selflessness that you both enact every day, it can subtly but radically change the world. It has mine.

INTRODUCTION

Sport and the Field of Performance

Montreal, Canada: A crisp autumn wind ruffles the mesh of an outdoor basketball net. On the asphalt court below the hoop, a group of teenagers play an informal half-court basketball game.

Tokyo, Japan: A coach sits on a bench in a mostly empty ice rink. On the ice, the blades of skates crackle as a dozen figure skaters complete warm-up laps before their training session.

Sydney, Australia: The buoys of seven lane ropes float on the surface of still water in an indoor pool. A horn blares, and eight swimmers dive into the water to start their race.

Cairo, Egypt: Blue mats cover an arena floor. In the middle of one sets of mats, two competitors wear Gis with black belts. With their arms held out in front of their bodies, they circle one another in a judo match.

Cape Town; South Africa: The seating area of a stadium is packed with people. On the field below, all twenty-two players are aware of the position of the rolling ball in a football game.

From pick-up basketball games and recreational figure skating lessons to amateur swim meets, elite karate matches, and professional football games, sporting occasions abound in the early twenty-first century. Indeed, apart from extraordinary circumstances such as global pandemics or major international conflicts, contemporary sport performances take place nearly every day of the week in locations around the world.[1] This is a book about such performances. More specifically, this is a book that examines sport through the lens of performances and theorizes performance through the lens of sport. How can critical language developed in the field of performance studies

DOI: 10.4324/9781003275879-1

facilitate analysis of gestures and movements in sport? How can performance methods help us better understand the individual, social, and cultural impacts of sports' events? Can studying sport illuminate new or previously undertheorized facets of performance?

Guided by these questions, the objectives of this book are three-fold. First, the book endeavours to advocate for the study of sport in the fields of theatre and performance studies, and to demonstrate how the critical language and methods of performance help illuminate the manifold impacts of the practices, activities, and events of sport. Second, the book introduces new critical language that was originally developed in conjunction with sport but is also designed for cross-genre performance analysis. In introducing novel terminology, the book aims to simultaneously facilitate analysis of sport performances and to show how the study of sport can contribute to the fields of theatre and performance studies. Third, the book endeavours to investigate the epistemological, affective, and socio-political effects of sport performances and to illuminate how sport performances influence, and are influenced by, their historical conditions.

The Starting Line: Sport and the Field of Performance

In 1958, Gene Kelly danced alongside sport legends Edward Villella, Dick Button, Mickey Mantel, Sugar Ray Robinson, and Johnny Unitas on an *Omnibus* television episode titled "Dancing: A Man's Game" (Graham). As part of the performance, Kelly welcomes Sugar Ray Robinson on stage and asks, "Sugar, what's the most important thing a boxer's got to have?" (Graham). With a smile and a playful tap on the shoulder, Sugar replies, "Rhythm man. Rhythm" (Graham). Facing the camera, the two men begin to tap dance, the pitter-patter of their steps in perfect time with one another. As the men dance, the program cuts away to pre-recorded split-screen clips. On the left side of the frame, an athlete performs a sport specific skill; on the right of the screen, a dancer performs the same skill with no equipment. The first of these clips features baseball player Mickey Mantle catching and then throwing an imaginary baseball in a stadium while a dancer performs a similar movement pattern on a stage. The men both jump into the air and extend their arms away from their bodies. Mantle reaches above his head while the dancer extends his hands so that they are parallel to the ground. Upon landing, both men rock their weight backwards, shuffle their feet, and cock their right arms behind their bodies. A moment later, they shift their weight forward and "throw" an imaginary ball toward the camera. The program then cuts back to Robinson and Kelly tap dancing alongside one another.

The similarities between both sets of men's movement patterns in this sequence would be relatively unremarkable if it were not for the fact that baseball and boxing are frequently conceptualized as belonging to a different cultural domain than jazz dance. Indeed, as the title of "Dancing: A Man's Game" suggests, one of the aims of Kelly and Robinson's routine was to unsettle commonly held mid-twentieth century distinctions between the realms of sport and dance, wherein the former was popularly associated with masculinity and manhood and the latter was not. While there have undoubtedly been important shifts in the nearly 70 years since "Dancing: A Man's Game" was produced, the cultural domains of sports and the performing arts are still frequently perceived as distinct and sometimes opposing spheres of production wherein participation in, affiliation with, or affinity for the performing arts frequently functions to signify a different set of interests, values and beliefs than participation in, affiliation with, or affinity for sports. I acknowledge such commonly held distinctions but take similarity rather than difference as the starting place for this project.

Neither Gene Kelly nor I are the first persons to recognize the links between sports and other fields of cultural production. The intellectual and disciplinary antecedents of this book can in part be traced to early twentieth-century theatre artists and cultural critics who queried the links between the realm of sports and theatre. Bertolt Brecht, for instance, argued that theatre had lost touch with its public and might learn from people's engagements with sport ("Emphasis on Sport"; Antonin Artaud compared the training of actors and athletes ("An Affective Athleticism"); Jacques Lecoq drew from his training as a physical educator to inform his physical theatre model (Evans); and Roland Barthes queried the aesthetic, social, and political dimensions of sport (*What is sport?*). In addition to such works, theories from early and mid-twentieth-century sociologists and anthropologists provided important frameworks for thinking about how sport crosses and intersects with different domains of cultural production. For example, Johan Huizinga examined the importance of play as a cultural phenomenon (*Homo Ludens*); Milton Singer introduced the term *cultural performance* to examine occasions demarcated from everyday life (*When a Great Tradition Modernizes*); Kenneth Burke theorized ritual dramas as the hub of human action (*The Philosophy of Literary Forms*); Clifford Geertz introduced the concept of deep play ("Deep Play"); Marcel Mauss examined bodily movement patterns across social domains ("Techniques"); and Pierre Bourdieu theorized sport in relation to his conception of habitus (*Distinction*). These works had important influences on the study of sport but resulted in limited cross-disciplinary analysis of sport and performing arts in the early and mid-twentieth century.

The emergence and development of performance studies in the 1960s and 1970s prompted increased pollination between academic fields such as theatre, anthropology, cultural studies, and linguistics. Works by Erving Goffman, Richard Schechner, Victor Turner, and John MacAloon attended to sport alongside other performance genres such as ritual, theatre, music, dance, play, and games, and laid the foundation for studying sport through the lens of performance.[2, 3] These studies also set a precedent for articles by Sally Ann Ness, who examined movement patterns across performance genres, Abigail Feder, who queried the performance of femininity in figure skating; and Kim Marra, who used auto-ethnography, performance, and horseback riding to make a historiographical intervention in studies of nineteenth-century women's equestrianism.[4] Despite such projects, however, sport remained outside the nuclei of performance studies theories, methods, and case studies in the twentieth century. To this end, while several widely used field surveys mention sport, none dedicated an entire section or chapter to the study of sport and performance, and there were no major performance studies theories or methods that were conceptualized for application to sport specifically.[5] In the early twenty-first century, this began to shift. A surge of articles related to sport and performance began to appear; examples include: Yasmine Marie Jahanmir's examination of the female Olympic swimmers who were cast in the New York World's Fair music, dance, and swimming extravaganza; Gary Alan Fine and Harvey Young's analysis of chess as sport performance; Natalie Alvarez's investigation of the intersection between simulation, theatricality, and diving in association football; Daniel Larlham's consideration of the cultural and aesthetic qualities of soccer performances; and Shannon Mazer's analysis of the similarities between the sphere of American politics and professional wrestling. [6,7] In addition to such chapters and articles, Jennifer Kokai released *Swim Pretty: Aquatic Spectacles and the Performance of Race* in 2017, Eero Laine published *Professional Wrestling and the Commercial Stage* in 2016, and three edited collections—on the topics of performance and professional wrestling, sport performances and politics, and depictions of sport in drama—were published between 2016 and 2022.[8] In this project I build from these rich streams of thought on sport and performance to develop a sustained, cohesive, framework for studying sport through the lens of performance.

The First Hurdle: Terms and Phenomena Part I—Sport

S*port* and *performance* share a common feature: they are both terms with multiple possible referents. It is, therefore, important to clarify how I am using these words. From the Norman French term *disport*—meaning "diversion from serious duties; relaxation, recreation; entertainment, amusement" ("disport")—the English word *sport* was first used to refer to "senses relating to play, pleasure, or entertainment" ("sport, n1") in the early fifteenth century. Over time, the term's meaning began to shift, and by the late nineteenth century, the relationship between *sport* and "an activity involving physical exertion and skill, especially one regulated by set rules or customs in which an individual or team competes against another or others" ("sport, n.1"), was beginning to stabilize. In contemporary common usage, the scope of the term can also be expanded to describe a field of socio-cultural production that includes people (athletes, coaches, officials, administrators), institutions (teams, organizations, federations), infrastructures (buildings, transport), and networks (leagues, circuits, finances, communications).

Importantly, however, *sport* is not an ideologically neutral term. The activities of sport—as well as the field and the word—have been, and continue to be, shaped by complex matrices of power structures and socio-political flows. Sport historians and sociologists frequently argue that organized sports emerged in England and the United States in the nineteenth and early twentieth centuries.[9] But, as I outline in the first chapter, the standardization and organization of activities as well as the popularization of the link between sports and competition was deeply enmeshed in power structures and majoritarian ideologies. For example, the forces of western imperialism played a key role in the early history of modern sport: settlers frequently appropriated and codified the activities of Indigenous peoples and also supplanted sporting activities in colonized territories.[10] Similarly, the early history of sport was strongly influenced by patriarchy and its associated ideologies. Most activities that are recognized as sports were created or developed by and for men, and from marathon running in the early and mid-twentieth century to ski jumping in the early twenty-first century, women have frequently had to battle for access, participation, and recognition.[11] This is not to suggest that the genealogy of sport should only be understood through top-down models of power. The field of sport is a domain of continuous negotiation, and there are innumerable instances of multidirectional influence. The early history of cricket in India, for example, may be inextricably bound with English imperialism, but in the twenty-first century, Indian cricket has its own, distinct, national culture, and the country is an important agent in international cricket.[12] The flows of power within the field of sport do, however, signal the charged power matrices that shaped, and continue to shape, sport—the word, the groupings of activities, and the field of cultural production.

The long entanglement between networks of power and the field of sport has led some humanities scholars to utilize alternative terms, often with the aim of broadening conventional understandings of the word. In the introduction *Sporting Performances,* for example, volume editor Shannon Walsh explains the use of the term *sporting* within the volume, noting that the term the term "invokes the playfulness involved in training and exercising, but … avoids a strict interpretation of sport" (2). Despite its history, however, *sport* remains the most common English-language term for naming competitive activities that involve the execution of physical skills. As such, I employ the *sport* throughout this book, and while I refine my understanding of the term in the first chapter, I begin with a broad notion of *sport* to refer to a range of human activities that commonly involve the enactment of physical skills or the expenditure of physical energy, that organize action in accordance with rules or codes, and that commonly feature competition between participants. I also use the term to refer to the areas of technique, fields of practice, and events connected to such activities as well as the field of socio-cultural production related to these activities.

Hurdle 2: Terms and Phenomena 2—Performance

As with *sport*, the term *performance* has many meanings. In everyday usage, the term can be used to denote a range of related, but distinct, phenomena including cultural events such as theatre or dance performances and individual skill enactments, as in an actor or dancer's performance. In the academic field of performance studies, the scope of the term's application is even more expansive. As Richard Schechner, "The one overriding and underlying assumption of performance studies is that the field is open. There is no finality to performance studies, either theoretically or operationally" (Schechner, *Introduction*, 1). One of the effects of the openness of performance studies is that the field is comprised of many different branches, several of which examine different types of performance from occasions to embodied enactments to discourse to facets of identity. Following the interdisciplinary impulse of the field, I also examine different kinds of sport performances. It is, therefore, helpful to take a brief tour of the different usages of *performance* as well as to clarify how I will employ related terms throughout the book.

In one branch of performance studies, the word performance is used to refer to cultural occasions that are framed, or bracketed, from everyday life; such occasions are often referred to as "events". As Marcela A. Fuentes argues, in the early twenty-first century "performance event" is frequently employed to "to differentiate framed, live cultural productions, from quotidian notions of performance, such as gender identity and national belonging, which are not enclosed within a specific space-time continuum" (26). Drawing from the work of scholars including Milton Singer, Victor Turner, Richard Schechner, Diana Taylor, and Erika Fischer-Lichte such events are usually conceptualized as "particular instances of cultural organization" (Singer xii) that include common characteristics such as the bracketing of time (performances have beginnings and endings), the segmentation of space (performances usually take place in "marked off" spaces), a special value assigned to objects (an object that might have little monetary or practical value in "everyday life" such as a soccer ball or a theatre prop which might have an important role and/or significant value within the world of the performance, and the sequencing of embodied action during the occasion.[13] My understanding of performance occasions draws from these conceptualizations but distinguishes between different types of cultural organization. In their conceptualizations of performance events, scholars have frequently implied or emphasized spectator-performer co-presence.[14] Spectator-performer co-presence, however, poses a challenge for performance genres like sport. While spectators are integral to professional and elite sporting events, recreational, and amateur sports are not predicated on the presence of spectators. Recreational basketball, hockey, and baseball games, for example, often take place without spectators. In fact, I participate in multiple organized recreational basketball leagues where spectators are seldom present. These games have all the elements of a performance: they bracket time, segment space, and organize sequences of embodied action during the occasion, but they do not imply or require audience members. Similarly, competitive elite and professional sports frequently include spectators, but can, in fact, proceed without co-present audience members—a fact that was evinced during the COVID-19 pandemic where thousands of sport performances took place with no spectators in the stadium.[15] To precise between occasions with spectators and those without, I use the term "activity" to refer to instances of cultural organization where spectators are not integral to the performance and "event" to denote instances of cultural organization where spectator-performer co-presence is integral to the occasion.

In another branch of performance studies, *performance* can be used to refer to collections of specialized and everyday behaviours and actions. Here, the term *practice* is often employed, as in the practices of ballet, piano, taekwondo, walking, or cooking. There is not, however, a single, agreed-upon, conceptualization of the scope of *practice*. As Theodore Schatzki suggests, most "thinkers who theorize practices, conceive of them … as arrays of activity" (Schatzki et al. 11), and while there is an emergent body of work that examines non-human activities, many scholars understand practices as "arrays of *human* bodily activity" (Schatzki et al, emphasis added). One of the points of divergence amongst definitions, however, is whether, and how, the term should address the mediation between embodied knowledges, collections of behaviours and actions, and individual instances of enactment.[16] To help delineate related phenomena, I follow Ben Spatz's notions of *technique* and *practice*. Building from a range of scholars—including Marcel Mauss and Michel Foucault—Spatz proposes that technique is a is a type of knowledge that "moves across time and space" (38) is "deeply influenced but not entirely determined by social power" (38) that "interacts in and through specific bodies and moments" of enactments (38). In contrast, he uses practice to refer to concrete instances of human bodily enactment. He explains, "If we look at chunks of human life bounded in time and space, we are looking at practices. If we look instead at the transmissible knowledge that links such chunks together across time and space, we are looking at techniques" (45). The distinction is useful for differentiating between areas of embodied knowledges (areas of performance technique) and collections of concrete bodily skills (performance practices).

In yet more branches of performance studies, additional types of performance are theorized. Influenced by the field of linguistics, and more specifically by the work of J.L. Austin, *performance* can also be used in relation to utterances. In this framework, utterances (performatives) can manifest social actions. Judith Butler drew from this conception of performativity to analyze how gender is produced in and through discourse and bodily repetition. This, in turn, lay the groundwork for examining socio-culturally coded behaviours and how they relate to performances of areas of identity such as gender, ethnicity, religion, or nationality. Following this genealogy, I use *performative* as a noun that refers to a specific category of utterance and *performativity* to indicate socio-cultural coded behaviours. As noted at the beginning of this section, *performance* can also be used to refer to the enactments of a specific individual or group: his performance, her performance, their performance. Falling within the purview of everyday understandings and usage, this deployment of the term has received less critical engagement than others within the field. But it is important because it crosses domains and scholarly fields from business to health sciences to the performing arts. Moreover, *sport performance* is commonly used in the fields of health, fitness, business, and government to refer to the evaluation or improvement of an individual or group's sporting enactment. As such, there are instances where I use the term in the possessive to refer to behaviours that have been enacted by an individual or group (her performance; their performance).

As Diana Taylor writes, "The many uses of the word performance point to the complex, seemingly contradictory, and at times mutually sustaining or complicated layers of referentiality" (3). This referentiality risks confusion between phenomena, but I see it as an opportunity to forge connections within and across socio-cultural fields. Cultural occasions like dance, theatre, and sport are rife with different types of performance. In the case of sport, there are the embodied practice and physical cultures of specific sports. There are the concrete enactments of athletes, who perform skills such as sprinting, skating, throwing, or kicking. There are the culturally coded behaviours of coaches, officials, and audience members, whose conscious and unconscious actions manifest a range of possible identities and affiliations from gender to nationality. And, there are sporting occasions themselves, as framed socio-cultural activities. Certainly, it is important not to conflate phenomena. An athlete's individual play in gridiron football is obviously distinct from a game of gridiron football. But it is precisely because the domain is filled with so many types of performance that the critical language and methods of performance studies are so well suited for the study of sport.

A Strategic Move: Critical Interventions

In the late twentieth century, Richard Schechner urged scholars to expand their conceptualization of performance to include a broad spectrum of framed and/or displayed human behaviours (*Performance Theory*). While this call to action has strongly influenced the interdisciplinary impulse of performance studies and prompted important cross-disciplinary investigations, sport has remained under-theorized in the field. In particular, there is a dearth of critical language and framework specifically developed for the study of sport. To begin to address this gap, in this book I introduce and develop three new critical concepts for performance research: a new conceptualization of *performance genre* (Chapter 1), which considers the material relations between activities in concrete historical contexts; the concept of *formation* (Chapter 2), which attends to the patterning of individual behaviour in specialized areas of physical culture; and the concept of *configuration* (Chapter 2), which examines the structuring of interpersonal behaviours during performance occasions.

In introducing these terms, I have three objectives. The first is to offer a set of performance-based concepts that emerge in specific relation to sports. Clifford Geertz' concept of "deep play" arose from Geertz' study of Balinese cockfights and Richard Schechner has examined sport alongside theatre, games, ritual, and play (*Performance Theory*). Overall, however, there is a scarcity of performance-based concepts that have been formulated in direct relation to sports. While I develop these concepts in direct relation to sports, however, they are intended for application in a range of performance genres, including theatre, dance, game, circus, and music. Following this, the second objective of introducing these terms is to demonstrate how approaching performance through the lens of sport can prompt the creation of innovative critical tools intended for cross-genre analysis. The third objective of the introduction of these concepts is to facilitate rigorous examination of sport performances and to use these terms to reveal how sport performances co-articulate the socio-political conditions of their emergence and practice. While it is beyond the scope of this project to outline all the contours of this co-articulation, one of central threads that runs throughout this project that twenty-first century sport performances are not merely products of existing ideologies or social structures; the practices, activities, and events of sport simultaneously shape and are shaped by their socio-political conditions.

The Playing Field: Scope, Methods, and Materials

Today, sport performances take place in locations all around the world, and as such, there are thousands—if not millions—of potential case studies and examples. Aiming to offer a framework for understanding the relationship between sport and performance and to also investigate the effects of actual sport performances, the scope of this project has two interconnected temporal spheres. The first broader sphere examines the areas of technique, practices, and occasions of sport from 1850 to the present while the second narrower scope focusses on sporting enactments and occasions in the twenty-first century. The expansive scope offers the necessary context to trace the long and frequently travelling genealogies of areas technique, practices and activities while the narrower sphere facilitates an investigation of contemporary sport performance.

The geographical parameters of this book's scope are also two-fold. As sport sociologists and historians have traced, the consolidation organized sport—as a historically specific grouping of activities and events—began to take place western Europe, the United Kingdom, the United States, Canada, and Australasia and moved to locales throughout the globe in the eighteenth, nineteenth, and early twentieth centuries.[17] The larger geographical scope of this project, then, includes all six continents where sports have been, and are, enacted from 1850 to the present: Asia, Oceania, Africa, North America, South America, and Europe. The narrower sphere focusses on sport performances in specific territories but understands these enactments within the broader twenty-first century global sports' ecology. As with other domains of cultural production, the international character of sport was impacted by twentieth-century globalization, broadly understood as accelerated processes of worldly connections and integrations between persons, economies, businesses, governments, and cultures. In particular, one of the effects of globalization was that it lubricated the flows between local, national, and international sport performance ecologies: professional leagues compete across national borders, impacting civic infrastructures such as the construction of stadiums; policies authorized by international sport federations influence national regulations which impacted civic and local rulebooks; telecommunication technologies broadcast sporting events to disparate locations, allowing audience members in Brazil, Sweden, and Japan to watch football games hosted in Qatar. As such, the geographic parameters of the overall project do not focus on a single nation or territory. Rather, I situate the context of each case study in relation to local, national, and transnational circuits. And, importantly, I do so from my own geographic position on the globe, as an athlete, researcher, and author who has mostly lived and worked in the nation-state of Canada, and, therefore, has mostly experienced sport from a north-western worldly vantage point.

Within these temporal and geographic scopes, there are the sport performances themselves. Some sport performances involve a single participant: a snowboarder gliding through a training run, a water polo player practicing their eggbeater kick. Other sport performances—youth baseball competitions or professional football matches—include dozens, hundreds, or even thousands of the participants. Each of these performances emerges from and contributes to a complex set of genealogies, from the history of areas of techniques and practices to the development of a sporting activity's rules to the socio-cultural context of a specific sporting event. To gather materials for research, I follow performance studies scholars such as Diana Taylor, Joseph Roach, and Carrie Noland, all of whom assert that knowledges, histories, and memories are transmitted through multiple systems, including the digital, the visual, the archival, and the bodily.[18] In particular, I follow Taylor's conceptualization of the repertoire to attend to the embodied dimensions of sport genealogies. For Taylor, archival memory "exists as documents, maps, literary texts, letters, archaeological remains, bones, videos, films CDs, all those items supposedly resistant to change" (19) while the repertoire "enacts embodied memory: performances, gestures, orality, dance, singing – in short all those actions usually thought of as ephemeral, nonreproducible knowledge" (20). Attention towards multiple types of knowledges is critical for understanding sporting performances, which emerge from and produce an array of happenings and remnants.

Multiple types of knowledges are also key for acknowledging the interplay between sport and broadcast technologies. Every spectator gathered in a gymnasium, a pool, a rink, or a stadium has a unique experience that they perceive as singular; at the same time, sport is inextricably linked to televisual, recording, and digital technologies. Professional and elite sporting events are frequently broadcast and recorded, and these recordings are replayed and excerpted. Competitive and recreational sports, too, are frequently filmed for archival, strategic, or personal purposes. In each chapter, then, I attend to a range of modes of knowledge transmission and draw from resources and materials, including photos, newspaper reports, and broadcasts; archival materials such as policy documents, rulebooks, programmes, and historical records; materials that examine issues related to sport performances, such as newspaper interviews, podcasts, magazine commentaries, and journal articles; and digital materials such as tweets and YouTube videos. I also draw from my own experiences with sports as an athlete, spectator, coach, and administrator. Growing up, I was a multi-sport athlete who participated in a range of sports from competitive swimming to soccer to track and field. Eventually, I specialized in basketball and played high school, university, and professional basketball. Since I stopped playing competitively, I have coached and administrated youth and adult basketball and have continued to play recreationally. I am also an active sport spectator. While these experiences are most obviously incorporated into the second chapter, my life-long participation in sports informs my research throughout, and where appropriate and possible, I draw from my lived experience.

Even in a book-length project, it is not possible to cover the full spectrum of sport performances. Nevertheless, I aim to investigate a range of different vectors of sport, including team and individual sports, different levels of competition (recreational, competitive, elite), professional and non-professional sports. I also endeavour to examine the intersection between sport performances and a range of participant demographics including gender, race, ethnicity, and nationality. To do so, I examine five sporting case studies: women's doubles' badminton at the Olympic Games, the genealogy of women's basketball practice, Canadian hockey audiences, the development of gridiron football in the United States and injuries in the contemporary National Football League, and the emergence of the butterfly stroke in international competitive swimming and the performance of Syrian-refugee Refugee Olympic team swimmer Yusra Mardini. Building from the impulse of performance studies—which does not does not champion a single method, but rather draws together a range of approaches to address the relationship between performances and their personal, embodied, social, cultural, and political effects—I utilize a range of methods as appropriate for each case, including phenomenological approaches to the study of bodily movement, archival interpretation, feminist analysis, cultural materialism, media analysis, affect theory, and close reading of policy and regulatory documents.

Gameplan: Chapter Summaries

Two connective through-lines guide the ordering of chapters. The first involves the theoretical progression of concepts: chapter one proposes an approach to *performance genres*; Chapter 2 introduces the key terms *configuration* and *formation*; and Chapters 3, 4, and 5 expand and apply these terms. The second through-line involves a progressive widening of scope. Because sport has yet to be extensively examined in the field of performance studies, the first chapter is distinct from the chapters that follow. In chapter one, I examine the relationship between sporting activities and events within the performance genre of sport. Building from this, I, hone-in on the patterning of practice for individuals (athletes) in Chapter 2 to the sequencing of interpersonal behaviours (athletes and audience members) in Chapter 3 to action sequences involving multiple groups of participants (athletes, audience members, event staff) in Chapters 4 and 5. For the purposes of clarity, each chapter begins with the discussion of a theory or critical concept and concludes with a case study.

The first chapter proposes an approach to performance genres and analyzes the performance genre of sport. More specifically, I put Caroline Levine's distinction between form and genre and Deleuze and Guattari's theory of assemblage in conversation with the genealogy of theories that examine the formal features of performance occasions. This leads me to propose a model for examining performance genres as recognizable groupings of activities and events that arise from meaningful sets of relations between phenomena in specific historical contexts. Applying this model to sport, I outline four of the meaningful relations that connect the performance phenomena within the performance genre of sport in the early twenty-first century. To demonstrate how the performance genre of sport influences specific sport performances, I turn to the match-fixing scandal that took place during the women's doubles' badminton tournament at the 2012 Summer Olympic Games in London. Through an analysis of this case study, I aim to demonstrate how genre can play an important role in shaping the socio-political and gendered effects of specific sport performances and to illuminate how patriarchal and western logics influenced the disqualification of eight female badminton players

In Chapter 2, I combine the critical tools and methods of performance studies with practice theory to introduce two new critical terms: *configuration*, which analyzes the traditions, conventions, rules, and laws that stitch together sequences of actions and behaviours during performance activities; and *formation*, which attends to the effects of the patterning of behaviour in specialized areas of embodied practice for individual bodies. Using the concepts of configuration and formation, I examine the genealogy of women's basketball in Canada and the United States. More specifically, I trace the emergence of the principle of the vertical plane, the concept that every basketball player has access to the space within an imaginary cylinder that extends around their torso, above their head, and below their feet. Building from this, I draw from Iris Young' theorization of modalities of feminine bodily comportment to analyze one of the basketball skills that is patterned by the principle of the vertical cylinder, "squaring-up". In doing so, I demonstrate how the concept of the vertical plane, which originally arose in the context of modified women's basketball in the early twentieth century, may empower contemporary female basketball players.

In Chapter 3, I elaborate on the concept of configuration by applying it to the analysis of audience behaviours. Building from my theorizations in Chapter 2, I introduce my conceptualization of performance events as occasions where the behaviours and actions of two or more groups of participants are stitched together by multiple, overlapping configurations. To expand on this concept and to investigate the patterning of audience behaviours, I analyze the emergence and growth of the hockey audience configuration in Canada from the late 1800s to the present. This analysis culminates with a discussion of how recording and communication technologies are shaping new hockey audience practices in the early twenty-first century. To examine the effects of these new practices, I analyze Canadian audience enactments during the men's gold medal hockey game at the 2010 Winter Olympic Games. Drawing together multiple strands of argumentation, I suggest that hockey audience practices function to both maintain hockey's position in Canada's popular imaginary and to support the ideologies imbedded in the enactment of the game.

In Chapter 4, I examine sequences of activity that cross-cut activities within a performance genre and investigate the patterning of behaviours of multiple groups of participants. To do so, I adapt the concept of liminal mini-dramas—introduced by Martin Revermann—to introduce the category of injury mini-dramas in sport, or the conventional behaviours that follow serious sporting injuries. Applying this concept to the study of football in the United States, I demonstrate how personal risk and serious injury are constitutive elements of the genealogy of gridiron football. I then turn to contemporary NFL football games. Analyzing two incidents involving the Seattle

Seahawks, I illustrate how injury-mini dramas in American football shape the experiences of multiple groups of participants so that victory and injury are mutually constitutive elements of the league's affective scenes.

In the final chapter, I tie the conceptualizations of previous chapters together to trace the dynamic circuit that connects performance genres to the practices, activities, and events of sport. More specifically, I analyze the relationship between competitive swimming and the emergence of the butterfly stroke in the mid-twentieth century. Drawing from Carrie Noland's concept of gestural marks, I aim to explore how the butterfly stroke functions to make specialized training socially legible, and, how, in doing so, the stroke becomes inflected by the socio-economic conditions that make that training possible. To demonstrate the socio-political significance of the enactment of the butterfly, I analyze Refugee Olympic Team member Yusra Mardini's performance of the 100-metre butterfly at the 2016 Olympic Games in Rio and demonstrate how her participation in the Games was leveraged by the International Olympic Committee to bolster the ideology of Olympism.

Notes

1 For the effects of the novel coronavirus pandemic on sport, see: Tamir.
2 For specific works by these authors, see: Goffman, "Frame Analysis", Schechner, *Performance Theory,* Turner, "Liminal to Liminoid"; MacAloon, *This Great Symbol.*
3 In 1998, Robert Rinehart published *Players All: Performance in Contemporary Sport* in 1998. In the book, Rinehart draws together cultural theory, aesthetic theory, sociology, and anthropology to examine specific sport performances in the United States in the late twentieth century. While the book does technically examine sport and performance, its methods, approaches, and focus resonate far more strongly with sociology and literary theory than they do with theatre and performance studies, and the book has not been widely cited in the field
4 See: Feder, "A Radiant Smile from the Lovely Lady"; Marra", Riding, Scarring, Knowing"; Ness, "Understanding Cultural Performance".
5 For field surveys, see: Auslander; Bial; Fischer-Lichte; Levin and Schweitzer; Schechner and Brady
6 See: Alvarez, "Foul Play"; Fine and Young, "Still Thrills"; Larlham, "On Empathy; Jahanmir, "We Rule the Waves"; Mazer, Donald Trump Shoots the Match".
7 In addition to these articles, *TDR* published a critique of "Donald Trump Shoots the Match" and Mazer's response to that critique in volume 62.2. See: Warden et al; Mazer "Sharon Mazer Responds".
8 Kokai, *Swim Pretty,* Walsh, *Sporting Performances;* Laine and Chow, *Sports Plays;* Chow, Laine, and Warden, *Performance and Professional Wrestling.*
9 For more on the early history of sport, see: Eitzen and Sage; Elias; Dunning et al.; Riess.
10 For more on the intersections between imperialism and/or colonization and sport, see: Bateman; Brownell, *The 1904 Anthropology Days;* Brownell "Wushu"; Carrington; Hargreaves *Sport, Culture, Ideology;* Holt; Malcom.
11 For more on the history of women in sport, see: Hargreaves, *Sporting Females;* Hall, *Sport and Gender;* Messner and Sabo.
12 For more, on the history of empire and cricket, see: Malcom; Boria. For more on cricket in twenty-first century India, see: Bose; Nair.

13 For discussions of space, see: Schechner, *Performance Theory;* Turner, *From Ritual.* For discussions of time, see: Singer; Turner; MacAloon; For discussions of special value assigned to goods, see: Schechner. For a discussion of the sequencing of action, see: Schechner, *Performance Theory;* Taylor, *The Archive and the Repertoire;* Fischer-Lichte.
14 For more on spectator-performer co-presence, see: Fischer-Lichte, pp. 38–74; Phelan, 146–66.
15 For more on sporting events and spectatorship during the COVID-19 pandemic, see: Tamir.
16 For a discussion of terminological differences in the field of practice theory, see: Schatzki, pp. 1–23. See also: Spatz pp. 38–44.
17 For more, see: Eitzen and Sage; Dunning et al.
18 See: Taylor, pp. 1–50; Noland, pp. 1–18; Roach, pp. 1–37.

References

Austin, J. L. *How to Do Things with Words*, edited by J. O Urmson and Sbisà Marina. Seconded. William James Lectures Delivered at Harvard University in 1955. Cambridge, Massachusetts: Harvard University Press, 1975: 5

Alvarez, Natalie. "Foul Play: Soccer's 'Infamous Thespians' and the Cultural Politics of Diving". *Tdr (1988-)*, vol. 60, no. 1, 2016, pp. 10–24.

Artaud, Antonin. "From an Affective Athleticism (1935)". *Twentieth-Century Theatre: A Sourcebook*, edited by Richard Drain, Routledge, 1995, pp. 272–3, doi:10.4324/9780203214671.

Auslander, Philip. "Liveness". *Reading Contemporary Performance: Theatricality across Genres*, Meiling Cheng et al., editors, Routledge, 2016, 154, doi:10.4324/9780203103838.

Barthes, Roland. *What Is Sport?* Yale University Press, 2007.

Bateman, Anthony. *Cricket, Literature and Culture: Symbolising the Nation, Destabilising Empire*. Ashgate Pub, 2009, doi:10.4324/9781315574769.

Bial, Henry, editor. *The Performance Studies Reader*. 2nd ed, Routledge, 2007.

Majumdar, Boria. "Cricket in Colonial India". *Economic and Political Weekly*, vol. 37, no. 15, 2002, pp. 1449–50.

Bose, Mihir. *The Magic of Indian Cricket: Cricket and Society in India*. Taylor & Francis, 2006.

Brownell, Susan. *The 1904 Anthropology Days and Olympic Games: Sport, Race, and American Imperialism*. University of Nebraska Press, 2008.

———. "Wushu and the Olympic Games. Combination of East and West, or Class of Body Cultures". *Perfect Bodies: Sports, Medicine and Immortality: Ancient and Modern*, edited by Vivienne Lo, vol. 188; no. 188, British Museum, 2012.

Burke, Kenneth. *The Philosophy of Literary Form: Studies in Symbolic Action*. 3rd ed., University of California Press, 1974.

Butler, Judith. "Performative Acts and Gender Constitution: An Essay in Phenomenology and Feminist Theory". *Theatre Journal*, vol. 40, no. 4, 1988, pp. 519–31.

Bourdieu, Pierre. *Distinction: A Social Critique of the Judgement of Taste*. Harvard University Press, 1984.

Brecht, Bertolt. "Emphasis on Sport". *Brecht on Theatre: The Development of an Aesthetic*, edited and Translated by John Willett, Hill and Wang, 1964, pp. 6–10.

Carrington, Ben. *Race, Sport and Politics: The Sporting Black Diaspora*. Sage Pub, 2010.

Chow, Broderick, Eero Laine and Claire Warden, editors. *Performance and Professional Wrestling*, 2017.

"Disport, N". *OED Online*, Oxford University Press, www.oed.com/view/Entry/55101.
Dunning, Eric et al. *Sport Histories: Figurational Studies in the Development of Modern Sports*. Routledge, 2004, doi:10.4324/9780203497432.
"Sport, n.1". *OED Online*, Oxford University Press. *Oxford English Dictionary*, http://www.oed.com.proxy.lib.sfu.ca/view/Entry/187476.
Eitzen, D. Stanley and George Harvey Sage. *Sociology of North American Sport*. 7th ed., McGraw-Hill, 2003.
Elias, Norbert. "The Genesis of Sport as a Sociological Problem". *The Sociology of Sport: Selected Readings*, edited by Eric Dunning, London, 1971.
Evans, Mark. "The Influence of Sports on Jacques Lecoq's Actor Training". *Theatre, Dance and Performance Training*, vol. 3, no. 2, 2012, pp. 163–77, doi:10.1080/19443927.2012.686451.
Feder, Abigail M. "A Radiant Smile from the Lovely Lady: Overdetermined Femininity in 'Ladies' Figure Skating". *The Drama Review 38*, vol. 38, no.1, pp. 62–78.
Fine, Gary Alan and Harvey Young. "Still Thrills: The Drama of Chess". *TDR: The Drama Review*, vol. 58, no. 2, 2014, pp. 87–98.
Fischer-Lichte, Erika, et al. *The Routledge Introduction to Theatre and Performance Studies*. English Language, Routledge, Taylor & Francis Group, 2014, doi:10.4324/9780203068731.
Fuentes, Marcela A. "Event". *Reading Contemporary Performance: Theatricality across Genres*, Routledge, 2016, doi:10.4324/9780203103838.
Geertz, Clifford. "Deep Play: Notes on the Balinese Cockfight". *Daedalus*, vol. 134, no. 4, 2005, pp. 56–86, doi:10.1162/001152605774431563.
Graham, William and Gene Kelly. "Dancing: A Man's Game". *Omnibus*, 1958.
Goffman, Erving. *Frame Analysis: An Essay on the Organization of Experience*. 1st Northeastern University Press edition, Northeastern University Press, 1986.
Hargreaves, Jennifer, editor. *Sport, Culture, and Ideology*. Routledge, 1982.
———. *Sporting Females: Critical Issues in the History and Sociology of Women's Sport*. Routledge, 2002. www-taylorfrancis-com.ezproxy.library.ubc.ca, doi:10.4324/9780203221945.
Hall, Ann. *The Girl and the Game: A History of Women's Sport in Canada*. Second edition, University of Toronto Press, 2016.
———. *Sport and Gender: A Feminist Perspective on the Sociology of Sport*. University of Calgary, 1978.
Holt, Richard. "Cricket and Englishness: The Batsman as Hero". *International Journal of Sport History*, vol. 13, no. 1, 1996, pp. 48–70.
Huizinga, Johan. *Homo Ludens: A Study of the Play Element in Culture*. Maurice Temple Smith Ltd, 1970.
Laine, Eero and Brodrick Chock, editors. *Sports Plays*. Routledge, 2021.
Jahanmir, Yasmine Marie. "'We Rule the Waves': Athletic Labor, Femininity, and the Collective in Billy Rose's Aquacade". *Drama Review*, vol. 61, no. 3, 2017, pp. 112–31.
Kokai, Jennifer A. *Swim Pretty: Aquatic Spectacles and the Performance of Race, Gender, and Nature*. Southern Illinois University Press, 2017.
Larlham, Daniel. "On Empathy, Optimism, and Beautiful Play at the First African World Cup". *Tdr: The Drama Review*, vol. 56, no. 1, 2012, pp. 18–47.

MacAloon, Johm. *This Great Symbol: Pierre De Coubertin and the Origins of the Modern Olympic Games*. University of Chicago Press, 1981.
Marra, Kim. "Riding, Scarring, Knowing: A Queerly Embodied Performance Historiography". *Theatre Journal*, vol. 64, no. 4, 2012, pp. 489–511.
Messner, Michael A. and Donald F. Sabo. *Sport, Men, and the Gender Order: Critical Feminist Perspectives*. Human Kinetics Books, 1990.
Mazer, Sharon. "Donald Trump Shoots the Match". *TDR: The Drama Review*, vol. 62, no. 2, 2018, pp. 175–200.
———. "Sharon Mazer Responds to Warden, Chow, and Laine". *TDR: The Drama Review*, vol. 62, no. 2, 2018, pp. 216–19.
Mauss, Marcel. "Techniques of the Body". *Economy and Society*, vol. 2, no. 1, pp. 70–87.
Nair, Nisha. "Cricket Obsession in India: Through the Lens of Identity Theory". *Sport in Society*, vol. 14, no. 5, 2011, pp. 569–80.
Ness, Sally Ann. "Understanding Cultural Performance: 'Trobriand Cricket.'" *TDR (1988–)*, vol. 32, no. 4, 1988, pp. 135–47. *JSTOR*, doi:10.2307/1145894.
Noland, Carrie. *Agency and Embodiment: Performing Gestures/Producing Culture*. Harvard University Press, 2009.
Phelan, Peggy. *Unmarked: The Politics of Performance*. Routledge, 1996.
Riess, Steven A. *Sport in Industrial America, 1850–1920*. Harlan Davidson, 1995.
Roach, Joseph R. *Cities of the Dead: Circum-Atlantic Performance*. Columbia University Press, 1996.
Schechner, Richard. *Performance Theory*. Routledge, 2004 doi:10.4324/9780203426630
Schechner, Richard and Sara Brady. *Performance Studies: An Introduction*. 3rd ed, Routledge, 2013.
Schweitzer, Marlis and Laura Levin, editors. *Performance Studies in Canada*. McGill-Queen's University Press, 2017.
Singer, Milton B. *Man's Glassy Essence: Explorations in Semiotic Anthropology*. Indiana University Press, 1984.
Schatzki, Theodore R, et al. *The Practice Turn in Contemporary Theory*. Routledge, 2001.
Spatz, Ben. *What a Body Can Do: Technique as Knowledge, Practice as Research*. Routledge, Taylor & Francis Group, 2015.
Tamir, Ilan. "There's No Sport without Spectators – Viewing Football Games without Spectators during the Covid-19 Pandemic". *Frontiers in Psychology*, vol. 13, 2022, doi:10.3389/fpsyg.2022.860747.
Taylor, Diana. *The Archive and the Repertoire: Performing Cultural Memory in the Americas*. Duke University Press, 2003.
Turner, Victor. "Liminal to Liminoid, in Play, Flow, and Ritual: An Essay in Comparative Symbology". *Ce Institute Pamphlet – Rice University Studies*, vol. 60, no. 3, 1974, pp. 53–94.
Warden, Claire, et al. "Working Loose: A Response to 'Donald Trump Shoots the Match' by Sharon Mazer". *TDR: The Drama Review*, vol. 62, no. 2, May 2018, pp. 201–15.
Walsh, Shannon, ed. *Sporting Performances: Politics at Play*. Routledge, 2020.

1
PERFORMANCE GENRES, SPORT, AND MATCH-FIXING AT THE 2012 OLYMPICS

On July 31, China's Wang Xiaoli and Yu Yang and South Korea's Jung Kyung-eun and Kim Ha-na are set to play against each other in the final game of Group A's round-robin stage of the women's doubles badminton competition at the 2012 Summer Olympics in London.[12] The umpire introduces the two teams of players and signals for the match to begin. Typically, elite international badminton involves fast-paced swings that send the shuttlecock zipping through the air and extended rallies between teams. In the moments that follow, the performance does not unfold as expected. South Korean player, Kim, opens the match with a drifting serve. Wang lunges toward the shuttlecock but waffles on contact, earning the South Korean team their first point. On the next serve, Kim serves to Yang who half-heartedly swings her racket and bats the shuttlecock into the net. On her third serve, the shuttlecock does not clear the mesh. As play continues, the players' gestures remain slow, and their skill executions result in numerous errors. It appears as if both teams might be trying to lose the game. The scene would become part of the largest disqualification of athletes from an Olympic Games for match-fixing for sporting reasons in the twenty-first century.

Why would athletes at the biggest international sporting event in the world seem play to lose? Why does playing to lose matter in sports? The answers to these questions are rooted in the topic of sport, as a performance genre. In western philosophical thought, the concept of genre can be traced back to Plato and Aristotle, both of whom proposed taxonomies for categorizing artistic phenomena. Though Aristotle's and Plato's models differ, both are underpinned by the assumption that the process of categorization is external to phenomena: the act of classifying a performance as "theatre" identifies the features of that performance but does not affect the performance itself.

DOI: 10.4324/9781003275879-2

While the use of the term genre moved out of aesthetics and into a range of cultural and intellectual spheres, including education, rhetoric, linguistics, and law, the underlying assumption remained a relatively stable feature of genre theory until the mid-twentieth century. In the last 50 years, however, the relationship between genre and phenomena has been re-theorized. As Anis S. Bawarshi and Mary Jo Reiff concisely summarize:

> Genre has come to be defined less as a means of organizing kinds of texts and more as a powerful, ideologically active, and historically changing shaper of texts, meanings, and social actions … This view recognizes genres as both organizing and generating kinds of texts and social actions, in complex, dynamic relation to one another. (4)

Performance genres, then, are not simply analytical or descriptive categories; they are phenomena in and of themselves.

In this chapter, I propose a novel approach for studying performance genres. Placing Caroline Levine's distinction between form and genre in conversation with Gilles Deleuze and Felix Guattari's concept of assemblage, I develop an understanding of performance genres as historically recognizable groupings of activities and events that emerge from meaningful sets of relations between phenomena in specific historical contexts. I, then, apply this approach to the performance genre of sport. To demonstrate the interplay between the relations within the performance genre of sport and contemporary sport performances, I return to the match-fixing incident in the women's pairs badminton tournament at the 2012 Olympic Summer Games. In so doing, I evince the significance of the features of the performance genre of sport for contemporary performance and illuminate the insidious bind between code of conduct documents and the athletes' gender in the 2012 women's pairs badminton incident.

Performance: Forms and Genre

In performance studies, the term "genre" is frequently employed to describe groupings of performance occasions such as ritual performances, theatre performances, performance art performances, spectacle performances, or dance performances. Influenced by trends in early and mid-twentieth-century anthropology—wherein the study of broad, sometimes called "universal," categorizations were popular—scholars interested in cross-genre analysis have frequently theorized expansive occasion taxonomies. Milton Singer introduced the idea of *cultural performance* to describe moments of socio-cultural organization; Victor Turner theorized the categories of liminal and liminoid performance to distinguish between different types of occasion; and John MacAloon proposed a ramified performance type to examine the overlapping performance categories of spectacles such as the Olympic Games. In conversation with such models, Richard Schechner proposed a broad-spectrum approach to the study of groupings of performance. In his performance chart model, Schechner traced the similarities and differences between types of performance, arguing that sport, dance, theatre, music, game, ritual, and play "comprise the public performance activities of humans" (7). While all of these approaches use the term "genre" to refer to categories of performance, their interests in transhistorical patterns and arrangements indicate that these theories are closer to what Caroline Levine might call a theory of form.

In *Forms: Whole, Rhythm, Hierarchy, Network*, Levine differentiates genre from form, arguing that genres cluster "customary constellations of elements into historically recognizable groupings of artistic objects, bringing together forms with themes, styles, and situations of reception" (14), whereas forms are "defined as patterning, shapes, and arrangements, have a different relation to context; they can organize both social and literary objects, and they can remain stable over time" (13). For Levine, forms range from literary forms like the sonnet to socio-political arrangements like the prison cell. Levine's conceptualization of genre requires minor adjustment for application in performance studies. Working from the perspective of literature studies, Levine limits genres to "groupings of artistic objects" (13). Performance occasions such as sports, games, parades, and spectacles, however, do not easily fit into the confines of "artistic objects." For application in performance, then, it is useful to expand genres beyond the aesthetic dimension and to define performance genres as historically recognizable groupings of activities and events. In this framework, occasions such as the pentathlon in Ancient Greece, jousting competitions in High Middle Ages England, and Karate matches in twentieth-century Spain are connected by the form of physical contest, but each involves distinct groupings of activities and events in specific historical time periods.

Importantly, following Levine's definitions of the terms, a theory of form analyzes phenomena to identify trans-cultural and/or trans-historical patterns and arrangements, whereas a theory of genre examines the relationship between phenomena in specific historical contexts. As such, even though theorists frequently use the term "genre" to name their categories of performance, their formulations are often much closer to theories of form.[3] Indeed, while performance studies scholars have formulated many theories of form, there is a dearth of cross-disciplinary approaches for the study of performance genres, as concrete collections of activities and events. Beyond the similarities between patterns and arrangements, how and why do performance activities in specific historical situations get grouped together? What are the meaningful connections between major categories of performance in specific socio-historical contexts? Theories of form are not equipped to robustly answer these questions. This adds a layer of difficulty for thinking across categories of performance, for conducting comparative analysis, and for mapping the intersections, overlaps, and complexities of larger socio-cultural fields.

So, performance genres are distinct from performance forms. But, what is the character of groupings of occasions in specific historical situations? How do such groupings come into being? The concept of assemblage, theorized by political philosophers Gilles Deleuze and Felix Guattari, helps further theorize. Developed throughout their collaborations, Deleuze and Guattari "never formalized" assemblage as "a theory per se, but largely used it [the concept of assemblage] ad hoc throughout their work" (Nail 21), and there is no single, clearly articulated definition of the concept. Broadly, however, Deleuze and Guattari's assemblage is used to refer to heterogeneous constellations of bodies, objects, expressions, and forces that are in constant, dynamic, relation with one another. While "assemblage" is the common English translation of Deleuze and Guattari's concept, the authors' original writings employed the term "agencement," which is closer to "arrangement" in English.[4] This is important because Deleuze and Guattari emphasized the heterogeneity and relationality of assemblages (as opposed to the unity that might be implied by the verb, assemble). To this end, they suggested that the logic of assemblages is unlike that of organisms, where unity connects the parts to the whole. Instead, they argued that assemblages are connected by a multiplicity of relations that bring elements together for varying intervals of time.[5] As such, assemblages are emergent and contingent, with varied elements in constant, dynamic relation with one another.

As phenomena that are defined by the relations between groupings of varied occasions, performance genres are paradigmatic examples of assemblages. The performance genre of sport, for example, comprises a variety of heterogeneous activities and events: tennis matches, polo games, track and field competitions, etc. These occasions involve a mix of elements including (athletes, officials, audience members), practices (swimming, soccer, gymnastics), areas of technique (running, skating, jumping), discourses (rules, laws, utterances), objects (balls, pucks, skates), and physical infrastructures (courts, fields, pools, etc.). And, as I will later outline, the grouping of occasions within the performance genre of sport also contains power structures, ideologies, and imaginaries. Importantly, however, there is no unified logic that holds these elements together. There is no one purpose or connection that links the twenty-first-century activities of trampoline, weightlifting, and ski jumping. Nor is there an actor or set of actors who drive the logics of relations between activities. Certainly, contemporary governing bodies like the Global Association of International Sports Federations (GAISF) recognize established and new sports, but such recognition responds to concrete practices, activities, and events (rather than directing the creation of new activities). Moreover, the GAISF's influence is most directly related to elite, competitive, international sport, which is one of several branches within the genre. Indeed, the elements within the performance genre of sport are forged through multifaceted, dynamic relations between elements. The same can be observed for contemporary meta-genres such as theatre, dance, and music, all of which become recognizable groupings of activities and events in specific historical situations through matrices of forces and relations.

Drawing from the above, it is possible to further precise a definition of performance genres as groupings of activities and events that emerge from the meaningful sets of relations between activities and events in specific historical contexts, and wherein constituent heterogeneous components are not connected by a singular logic but rather by dynamic relations that continuously emerge, dissolve, and re-organize. In addition to describing the manifold character of performance genres, such a conceptualization captures the processual quality of performance. As Dwight Conquergood suggests, performance practices, activities, and events are emergent and processual, and it is therefore critical to shift from analyzing "static structures and stable systems with variables that can be measured, manipulated, and managed" to analyzing how "culture becomes transacted through performance" (83). Indeed, while performance occasions may have common patterns that stitch together gestures, movements, and sequences of action, the enactment of these patterns is not stable or static. The dynamic quality of assemblages, then, echoes the processual qualities of performance, which, in turn, resonates with the emergent quality of performance genres as phenomena that arise from the relations between concrete instances of enactment. Moreover, the concept of assemblage helps describe the materialization of performance genres. Put simply, while the *form* of a physical contest can be found in a range of cultures and historical contexts, the performance *genre* of sport, as a grouping of recognizable activities, did not precede the emergence of sports; it emerged from concrete activities and the relations between them (more on this below). The same is true for other contemporary performance genres: Broadway musical theatre, burlesque, and rap battles emerged from concrete activities in the nineteenth and twentieth centuries and are all recognizable clusters of activities in the early twenty-first century.

Studying Clusters of Activities and Events: The Performance Genre of Sport

In his discussion of literary genres, Stephen Owen argues that "the hinterlands of a genre are often contested territory" (1389) and that the act of defining genres can be "remarkably close legislation or border control" (1389). Indeed, engaging in a "counting" exercise is one of the risks of mapping the occasions within a performance genre. Does blackjack count as a sport? What about video games? Theatre sports? Show choir? There are instances where such lines of inquiry have important concrete stakes, as is the case when sport and the performing arts fall under the purview of different governance or financial structures. Intellectually, however, such questions are usually limited. Rather than asking whether a specific performance "counts" as a sport, it is far more productive to investigate the meaningful relations between the activities and events within the genre. To do so, it is important to acknowledge the core characteristics of performance genres as clusters of (1) historically situated (2) phenomena (3) that are constituted by dynamic relations between (4) activities and events in specific historical situations. Here, I take a broad scope that examines the performance genre of sport from 1850 to the present in Asia, Oceania, Africa, North America, South America, and Europe. While this scope is expansive, it reflects the coalescence of activities that began to take place in the mid-nineteenth century, which is key for understanding the currents that connect elements within the sporting assemblage. This scope also mirrors the international quality of the genre's development and its contemporary worldly character. My own vantage point, however, delineates the boundaries of analysis. As an athlete, coach, researcher, and author, I am not outside the performance genre of sport; I am, in fact, located within the assemblage, and my perspective is shaped by my lived experiences in the nation-state of Canada in the late twentieth and early twenty-first centuries. While I attempt to account for a range of angles and their associated knowledges, memories, and experiences, this contemporary, north-western, worldly vantage point shapes the parameters of my perspective.

To investigate the genre, I consulted a range of sources and compiled a list of occasions that are conventionally conceptualized as sport (see Appendix 1). I, then, formulated a series of questions intended to help identify meaningful relations between activities and events. I do not mean for these questions to be prescriptive. Rather, I endeavour to offer a starting place for analysis of the performance genre of sport and to provide a potential starting point for future cross-genre analysis. These questions were as follows:

1. What are the most significant processes or systems that forged and/or maintain connections between occasions within the performance genre of sport?
2. What are the areas of technique that pattern enactment during the occasions of sport?
3. What patterns (forms) influence the enactment of practice during sporting occasions?
4. How do forms and areas of technique intersect to shape the purpose of sporting activities for performers?
5. What are the similarities between activity configurations in the performance genre of sport?
   a. To what degree are segments of action or behaviours scripted, choreographed, or scored?

b. Are space and time primarily organized by rules, conventions, laws, or traditions? What role do officials play in the arrangement of time and space?
c. How do the performance activities conclude? What is the relationship between an activity's conclusion and its outcome? To what degree are the conclusion and the outcome pre-determined?

From these questions, I was able to identify several of sport's connective currents. For the purposes of clarity, I have clustered connective threads into four categories: historical processes and systems; forms; practices and areas of technique; relationships between activities.

Current 1: Historical Processes and Systems— Patriarchy and Western Imperialism

As sport sociologists and historians have demonstrated, the coalescence of the set of meaningful relations that resulted in the emergence of the performance genre of sport was the result of a matrix of intersecting currents, including urbanization, technological innovation, educational processes, socio-economic relations, professionalization of leisure activities, shifting international orders in the nineteenth and twentieth centuries, and the growth of capitalism.[6] As is the case with other assemblages, these relations are dynamic, constantly changing, dissolving, re-emerging, and intersecting with one another. Rather than attempting to trace the full ecology of ideologies and systems that run through the performance genre of sport, I highlight two particularly important currents: western imperialism and patriarchy. Sport historians and sociologists frequently suggest that modern sport emerged in England and the United States in the nineteenth and early twentieth centuries.[7] It is true that many activities that are contemporarily categorized as sport were first codified during this time in these locations: soccer was codified in the 1860s in England; Basketball was codified in the 1890s in the United States; badminton was codified in the 1890s in England; and association football was codified in England in the 1890s.[8] Critically, however, the association between the "codification" and "creation" or "development" of many these activities is the product of western imperialism and the logics of colonization. Through a process that has been described as "sportization" by sociologist Norbert Elias, some of the activities that are now known as sports did emerge from folk games that originated in western Europe and the United States.[9] Other activities, however, were codified by settlers who appropriated the activities of colonized peoples. The codification of lacrosse, for example, is commonly attributed to Canadian-settler William George Beers but the game had been played for hundreds of years by Indigenous peoples in the territories now known as North America.[10] Similarly, badminton and polo emerged in

India but were not widely recognized as "sports" until they were officially "codified" in England in the late 1800s.[11]

In addition to the appropriation and codification of Indigenous activities by colonizers, western imperialism also resulted in the spread of codified activities to colonized places. Focussing on the period from 1815 to 1914, Ben Carrington describes this process:

> European direct colonial rule dramatically increased from 35 to 85 percent of the world's surface. The two great imperial powers of that time, namely Britain and France, are also the two countries that did most to institute the national and international codes of sporting conduct and governance. This has led many historians to argue that sports are an example of western cultural diffusionism par excellence. Where the Empire went, so did the sports of the colonizers. (37)

This process has been the most extensively traced in relation to cricket. The codification of cricket began in the eighteenth century in England, and by the late nineteenth century, it was widely considered England's "national game."[12] As Dominic Malcolm argues, the adoption of cricket throughout the British empire was a complex process that was not homogenous across different countries (48–62). Nevertheless, by the late nineteenth century the game was played in countries throughout the empire, including India, New Zealand, and South Africa. A comment by Lord Harris in 1880 captures the perceived significance of the spread of cricket through British imperialism. He argued, "The game of cricket has done more to draw the Mother Country and the Colonies together than years of beneficial legislation could have done" (qtd. in Holt, 227). Importantly, this logic was not limited to cricket and the British empire, and a range of sporting activities were diffused across the globe through western imperialist processes.

The relations forged by these processes and logics bound together the elements of sport as a performance genre in the nineteenth and twentieth centuries and continue to do so in the twenty-first. The sport programme of the Olympic Games offers an indicative example of the continuing effects of western imperialist logics. In her examination of wushu, a Chinese martial arts activity, Susan Brownell argues, "The historical reality is that most of the sports on the Olympic programme were spread throughout the world through western colonialist and imperialist expansion, and they emerged out of the historical conditions that produced them." Writing about the 2006 Olympics, she notes "There are only two sports of clearly non-western origin on the Olympic-Games programme – Judo (Japan) and taekwondo (South Korea)" (64). In 2020 Olympic Games, the situation did not improve. The programme now includes the addition of one sport of clearly non-western origin, Karate; however, there has been an increase in clearly western origin sports, such as BMX biking and skateboarding, meaning that the ratio of western to non-western origin sports has increased rather than decreased. Importantly, as I demonstrate through my analysis of the match-fixing scandal in the women's badminton tournament at the 2012 Olympic Games, the logics of western imperialism also influence specific instances of sport performance.

In addition to western imperialism and colonialism, patriarchy played a critical role in the emergence of sport as a performance genre. As Ann Hall writes:

> The history of modern sport is a history of cultural struggle. Privileged groups in our society—seemingly by consent—are able to establish their own cultural practices as the most valued and legitimate, whereas subordinate groups (like women) have to fight to gain and maintain control over their own experiences and at the same time have their alternative practices and activities recognized as legitimate by dominant culture. (1)

Intersecting with numerous other important currents, including industrialization, urbanization, capitalism, the emergence of new class structures within countries, shifting notions of masculinity, changing gender roles, and the ideology of muscular Christianity, most of the activities that would become recognized as sports were created or developed by and for men.[13] As a consequence of these currents and the male control and enactments of sporting activities, many sporting activities were strongly associated with masculinity, manhood, and male relations, and while women actively sought and gained sporting participation in the late nineteenth and early twentieth centuries, the emergence of the performance genre of sport was primarily associated with men and was strongly infused with patriarchal ideologies.[14]

As with western imperialism and colonialism, patriarchy and the link between sport and masculinity has consistently been a key relation that connects practices, activities, and events to one another in the performance genre of sport. As Ann Hall writes, "Sport in our culture is still viewed by many as a 'masculinizing project,' a cultural practice in which boys learn to be men and male solidarity is forged" (1). The effects of this view are evinced by a range of examples, including the continued gender division of most competitive, elite, and professional sporting activities, the pay inequity between professional men's and women's sports, and the continued regulation of women's, non-binary, and trans-bodies in sports through sex and gender verification policies, uniform restrictions, and code of conduct documents, the latter of which I examine in the case study that concludes this chapter.

Current 2: The Form of Contest and The Purpose of Activities

The form of physical contest is common across sport performances. For athletes, this means that the key purpose of activities is to compete. In *Performance Theory*, Schechner argues that whether a performance is called "'ritual' or 'theatre' depends mostly on context and function. A performance is called theatre or ritual because of where it is performed, by whom, and under what circumstances" (130). In *Introduction to Performance Studies*, Schechner expands his original theorization and suggests that performances have eight primary functions: "to entertain; to make something that is beautiful; to mark or change identity; to make or foster community; to heal; to teach, persuade, or convince; to deal with the sacred and/or the demonic" (46). While sports do not easily fit into one of these eight categories, this is a useful framework for beginning to theorize the overall function of the performance event for spectators. In my conceptualization, I use "function" to think through the overall aims and effects of performance events and "purpose" to refer to the underlying objectives that stitch together participant behaviours. In a contemporary ritual such as a wedding, for example, the overall function of the event might be to mark the official union of two people, whereas the purpose of the civil servant is to coordinate, perform, and validate a prescribed sequence of behaviours.

Though not always explicitly stated, competition stitches together the conventions, rules, laws, and traditions that organize behaviours and sequences of action in each activity. The rules of soccer, for example, indicate the purpose of the game (to direct a ball between two posts more times than the other team directs the ball between two posts) and dictate what kinds of behaviours can be used to achieve this purpose (with the exception of the goalie, players cannot touch the ball with their hands). Importantly, competition orients performers toward each other and/or toward the objective of the competition: in judo, the athletes, who engage in direct physical contact, are oriented toward one another; in ski racing, the racers are oriented toward the finish line and toward time (or more specifically the time it takes to get to the finish line); in gymnastics, the competitors are oriented toward the execution of the perfect front aerial.

Current 3: Practices and Areas of Technique

Evidenced by *The Oxford English Dictionary's* definition of athletics as "[t]he practice of an activity requiring physical skill, strength, endurance, etc. often as part of a sporting competition" ("athletics, n"), the area of technique of athletics is often associated with the activities of sports. An instance of running, for example, is frequently considered an instance of athletics when it takes place in the context of a sporting activity. What emerges from my survey, however, is that practice in the activities of sports is structured by a range of specialized areas of technique, including (but not limited to) gymnastics, dance, acrobatics, athletics, equestrian, martial arts, sailing, and driving. Traditionally, participants in sporting activities are usually required to use multiple areas of the body to enact physical skills. In speed skating, for example, the skater does not only use their legs to skate; they also engage muscles in their torsos and swing their arms. Of course, the parts of a body are interdependent; my heart cannot execute the task of skating on its own, and my legs likewise cannot skate without my heart (or my lungs or my bones or my torso).

At the level of the individual, all instances of enactment—from sitting in a chair to doing a double-axel jump in a figuring skating competition—engage multiple areas of the body. Significantly, however, the patterning of behaviour that takes place in sporting activities tends to structure practice so that specialization connects a body's movements. An individual who is able to run in their daily life is likely able to run in the context of a race. But, to enact the purpose of a race and to run as fast as possible, specialized skills such as the lengthening of one's stride or the pumping of the arms is often utilized to complete the task. Specialization is more important in sports where multiple skills are enacted simultaneously; in hockey, for example, the execution of physical skills requires an athlete to execute simultaneously the skill of skating and the skill of holding and manoeuvring a hockey stick, whereas, in distance running, an athlete is only required to run, lowering the required level of specialization needed to participate. Nonetheless, the practices of hockey and marathon running are both structured by specialized areas of technique. It can, therefore, be noted that the practices of sport are structured by a range of areas of specialized technique. Practice is patterned so that observable, usually specialized, skills often involving multiple areas of the body are required to execute tasks.

Current 4: Relationships between Activities

The are several similarities between the conventions, traditions, laws, and rules that stitch together action in the performance genre of sport. These similarities are outlined below. Some of these connections may appear to be overly fastidious intellectual distinctions, but they are key for understanding the experiential similarities and differences between different kinds of performance. To participate in a performance that ranks performers based predominantly on luck is a distinct experience from participating in a performance that ranks performers predominantly based on skill execution. Importantly, however, the significance of characteristics varies during actual performances. Specific instances of sport may amplify, dampen or omit one or several of these features. Recreational sports, for example, frequently dampen the significance of competition, and stringent adherence to rules is often loosened, reducing the need for officials. In my recreational co-ed basketball league, there are no referees, and the games are self-regulated by players (a league convention that often causes interpersonal tension).

First, the activities of sport have a low degree of pre-determined, or scripted, behaviours. As with all performance occasions, conventions, rules, laws, and traditions organize time, space, and behaviours into sequences of action during sports. Soccer games, for example, begin with a kick-off and divide action into two 45 minutes halves. Within these broad segments of action, however, sports have a low degree of choreographed behaviours or actions. The activity configuration of soccer does not script what behaviours will be enacted during the two sequences of action; performers behave in relation to other participants, objects, and environmental factors such as the weather. Of course, the degree to which behaviours are scripted varies from activity to activity, but even in aesthetic sporting activities, such as half-pipe snowboarding or gymnastics, sequences of action and their outcomes are not predetermined. In a gymnastic floor routine, a single performer will attempt to execute pre-determined choreography, but their attempt will not necessarily be successful, and the judges' interpretation of their routine is unknown. So, while gymnastics and half-pipe snowboarding have a higher degree of moment-to-moment choreography than tennis, they have a far lower degree of pre-determined action than a scripted western theatre show or traditional ballet performance.

Second, the outcome of the activities of sport involves the ranking of performers based on the enactment of practice during the organized time of performance activities; activities conclude when it is possible to rank participants. There are two main modes of ranking that occur in the activities of sport. The first mode ranks performers by dividing them into two groups: winner(s) and loser(s). This mode of ranking is common in sports where performers compete directly against one another, such as in boxing, judo, lacrosse, and curling. The second mode ranks performers by placement; this is the case in activities such as marathons, swimming, javelin throwing, diving, bob-sledging, and BMX biking. In this second mode of ranking, ties may be acceptable, and it may be possible to have more than one winner. Ties may also be possible in sport performances that typically utilize the first mode of ranking if that performance is embedded in a meta-performance form such as a tournament. A regular season recreational league hockey game, for example, might end in a tie; however, each game in the regular season is positioned in relation to the overall season, which is the round-robin tournament, and all recreational hockey seasons often conclude with playoffs that determine a single, overall, winner. Importantly, unlike other contests, such as essay contests or award ceremonies, the activities of sport rank performers based on enactments that happen during the activity itself; this ranking takes place directly following the athlete(s)'s performance. In an activity where participants execute skills simultaneously (a marathon, a soccer game), the ranking will be the outcome of the competition. In an activity where competitors execute skills consecutively (weight lifting, snowboarding, rhythmic gymnastics), each performer's execution will be scored or recorded directly following their enactment.

Third, in sport, time and space are primarily organized by rules and officials are often embedded into the activity in order to ensure the enforcement and application of rules. Rules play an essential role in organizing time and space in the activities of sport, and there is often strict adherence to the rules; even in a game of recreational badminton, the shuttlecock is considered out of bounds if it crosses the court line. In instances of sport where competition is emphasized—competitive, elite, and professional sports, for example—officials are embedded into activities in order to ensure adherence to rules; however, officials are not essential to all branches of sporting activities. Adult recreational sporting activities, for instance, are sometimes self-officiated.

Finally, luck is not a primary factor in determining the outcome of the activities of sport. Luck plays a role in sports: the bicyclist benefits from an unexpected tailwind; the golf ball hits all four corners of the lip of the hole but, inexplicably, pops out; the player on the opposing lacrosse team has the best game of their lives. However, luck is not embedded into activities so it plays a central role in the ranking of performers. A single shot in golf may be influenced by luck, but over the course of a round that involves dozens of shots, the execution of physical skill plays a far greater role in the ranking of players than luck.

Match-Fixing in the Women's Badminton Tournament at the 2012 Summer Olympics

With a more robust understanding of performance genres, it is now possible to return to the case study and illustrate the complex intermingle between sport (the genre) and contemporary activities (sports). This chapter began with a description of a match between two teams of badminton players in the final round-robin game of the pairs' tournament at the London Olympics Games in 2012. As noted, as soon as the match began, both teams committed several errors on routine shots. Serves hit the net. The players seemed to intentionally direct the shuttlecock outside the court's boundaries. Later, the final match of the Group C stage took place between South Korea's Ha Jung-eun and Kim Ming-jung and Indonesia's Meiliana Juahari and Greysia Polii. The scene was strikingly similar: the players missed routine shots; the referee attempted to intervene; South Korea eventually won in two sets. Within hours of the two matches, the Badminton World Federation (BWF) organized a review panel to investigate. A day later, on August 1, 2012, the BWF announced that all eight athletes were disqualified from the Olympic tournament for breaking the BWF's code of conduct by "not using one's best efforts to win a match" and "conducting oneself in a manner that is clearly abusive or detrimental to the sport" (Walker & Siddique). This outcome was shaped by the form of contest, the ideology of fair play and its effect on the patterning of practice, and the power structures that continue to crosscut the performance genre of sport.

The Form of Contest, Or Why Playing to Lose Matters

While the importance of competition may be lessened in youth or recreational sports, the form of contest is paramount in elite sports, and, by extension, the implied purpose of sporting activities for athletes—to compete to win—is heightened. As such, when athletes play to lose, they unsettle the formal dimension of sport by undermining the competitive aspect of contest. In fields such as performance art, formal subversion is often lauded. But, in competitive, elite, and professional sports, this is rarely the case, and there are dense regulatory processes that attempt to maintain the competitive character of the contest form. These processes fall under the broad banner of match-fixing. Broadly, match-fixing refers to the intentional manipulation of a sporting activity which usually, but not always, affects the outcome of a competition. While all instances of match-fixing are connected to one another by the manipulation of sport competitions, match-fixing is not a unified concept or practice, and incidents can be grouped into two broad categories. The first category of match-fixing comprises instances motivated by gambling, betting, or corruption. In this category, third-party agents who are not directly involved in a sport competition influence individuals or groups that engage in match-fixing. These indirect agents might include gamblers, organized criminals, or political agents such as representatives from national governing bodies; an example of the latter category is the figure skating scandal at the 2002 Olympics in Salt Lake City, where the French skating organization was accused of exerting pressure on a French judge (Clarey). The second category of match-fixing encompasses the manipulation of a sport competition motivated by sporting reasons. In such instances, no third-party agents motivate the manipulation. Rather, the athletes or coaches manipulate a competition as a strategy or tactic; this is commonly called "tanking" or "throwing" a match. One example of this occurs in sport competitions where round-robin or league play precedes playoff rounds. In such cases, individuals or teams may manipulate a match to try and secure a more favourable situation in the playoffs. In competitive, elite, and professional sports, undermining the form of contest through match-fixing involving corruption, betting, or gambling is often considered a violation of ethical principles, rules, and sometimes laws. Instances of match-fixing for sporting reasons are also generally perceived sceptically, but responses are more varied and complex. As Salomeja Zaksaite argues, "the concept of manipulation may depend on the specificity of the sport: in some branches of sports the same acts can be considered as (punishable and illegal) manipulations, while in other branches of sports similar acts are just widespread tactics" (289).

The 2012 women's badminton incident is an example of match-fixing for sporting reasons. The Summer Olympics first introduced Badminton into its programme in 1992. From 1992 to 2008, Olympic badminton tournaments used a single elimination format; however, for the 2012 Olympic Games, the BWF changed the format to a combination of round-robin play and knock-out rounds. In the group stage, athletes competed in four pools. The top two seeds from each pool continued to the quarterfinal. For players, the format change was significant. In the single-elimination format, athletes must win each game to advance in the tournament. However, in the 2012 tournament configuration, teams could lose games in the group stage and remain in the tournament, and as teams reached the final stage, this meant that top competitors could choose to lower their energy expenditure or try to secure (what they considered to be) favourable playoff matchups by winning or losing the final game of round-robin play. In addition to the observable actions during games, post-game comments from players and coaches confirm the players' in-game actions. The South Korean coach, Sung Han-kook, argued, "The Chinese started this. They did it first. It's a complicated thing with the draws. They didn't want to meet each other in the semi-final" (Alleyne) He went on to say that the Chinese team's actions motivated his team's behaviour, arguing, "Because they don't want to play the semi-final against each other, so we did the same. We didn't want to play the South Korean team again" (Alleyne). In her defence, Yu, of the Chinese team, suggested that her team was trying to conserve energy. She said, "Actually these opponents really were strong. This is the first time we've played them and tomorrow it's the knockout rounds, so we've already qualified and we wanted to have more energy for the knockout rounds" (Alleyne). As I outline below, the rules of international badminton explicitly address "using one's best efforts," and despite the above explanations, the players actions were perceived negatively by tournament officials and the BWF, the latter of whom ultimately disqualified them from competition. The disqualification was supported by the members of the International Olympic Committee (IOC), and IOC spokesman Mark Adams praised the BWF's decision, stating, "Such behaviour is incompatible with the Olympic values" ("Played Disqualified"). These responses begin to suggest how the form of contest inflected the 2012 match-fixing incident.

Practices and Areas of Technique: Fair Play and the Patterning of Behaviour

The expectation that athletes will engage authentically in competition signals a long-standing tension between specialized areas of practice and athlete comportment in sport. From exaggerating the effect of player contact in field hockey to taunting opponents in gridiron football to complaining to officials in tennis, there is a range of behaviours that are not amongst the specialized practices of competitions but are, nevertheless, commonly performed in sporting activities. Historically, such behaviours have been managed through the ideology of fair play. "Fair play'" is a concept traceable throughout the history of sports in a range of times and places.[15] Variations of the concept can be found at the Ancient Olympic Games where athletes were expected to behave honourably in front of the gods (Sheridan 164). The concept, as we use it today, emerged in nineteenth-century Victorian Britain.[16] Universities and public schools in Britain employed sport as an integral part of their physical education programs and commonly believed sport exerted a positive influence on the physical and moral education of young men. In this context, fair play meant "more than simply adopting the norm of playing by the written rules of the sport, accepting what is prescribed and proscribed by the authorities" (Vamplew 857). It emphasized the importance of how athletes behaved during games and "denoted behaviour that was not specific in the written rules but which encompassed human virtues, such as self-discipline, modesty, generosity, tolerance, respect, and courtesy" (Vamplew 858). While this conception of "fair play" originated in Britain, it quickly gained traction across non-British nations, and in 1896, Baron Pierre de Coubertin adopted the term to build his idea of the Olympic movement. This functioned to further popularize and spread the ideology of fair play and its application in sport.

In terms of the development of rules in sport, the values of fair play began primarily as unwritten principles. These principles underpinned the teaching and behavioural expectations of a range of sports. Throughout the late nineteenth and early twentieth centuries, however, these unwritten principles were increasingly circulated through written materials. For example, golf handbooks often included an etiquette section before the rules, outlining appropriate behaviour during a game. We see this shift, too, in the evolution of Olympic documents. The original Olympic Charter, published in 1908, contained no comments about the behaviours of participants. The 1933 Charter, however, began with a page titled "Are you a Sportsman?" which asked a series of guiding questions about good sportsmanship for both players and spectators ("International Olympic Committee" 2).

General principles, however, did not foreclose the possibility of players breaking or bending the rules. As a result, rulebooks began including additional rules, and the ideology of fair play influenced the development of what sport philosophers call "regulatory" and "auxiliary" rules. Unlike constitutive rules, which provide the formal rules of play, including information about equipment and playing space, auxiliary rules pertain to conditions of an athlete's eligibility to participate in a sport competition and regulatory rules concern behaviours related to but independent from the constitutive rules (Vamplew 854–55). In early versions of soccer's rules, for example, there existed no penalty kick, as it was assumed that a gentleman would never intentionally commit a foul ("History of the Laws"). However, by 1881, it was clear that additional rules were needed to regulate players' behaviour, and penalty kick provisions were adopted ("History of the Laws"). Since the early nineteenth century, several regulatory rules were added to the rulebook, including an entire section devoted to fouls and misconduct that provide for "violent conduct," "spitting at an opponent or any other person," and "using offensive, insulting or abusive language and/or gestures" (Federation International de Football Association 41). As a result of the addition of rules throughout the nineteenth and twentieth centuries, by the late twentieth century, rulebooks frequently ran dozens, and sometimes hundreds, of pages long.

The continuous play section of the badminton rulebook is another example of regulatory rule expansion in sports. Although versions of badminton rules began circulating much earlier, the codification of badminton rules officially commenced with the Badminton Association of England's founding in 1893. Early versions of the rules did not contain a continuous play section; rather, the rules outlined basic constitutive rules, including specifications about the court and scoring (Badminton Association of England). In 1934, the International Badminton Federation was formed; however, it was not until the 1960s that a "continuous play" clause reached the rulebook (American Badminton Association, "The official rules"). The clause decreed that "play shall be continuous from the first service until the match be concluded" (American Badminton Association, "The official rules"). From 1962 to 1982, this clause was included under the "General" section of the rulebook. Eventually, however, "continuous play" became its own section in the handbook, and in 1992, the first year the Summer Olympic Games hosted badminton, the name of the continuous play section was changed to "Continuous Play, Misconduct, and Penalties" ("International Badminton Federation"). This version of the Laws itemizes four regulatory rules for players. The laws state:

18.7 A player shall not:
18.7.1 Deliberately cause suspension of play;
18.7.2 Deliberately interfere with the speed of the shuttle;
18.7.3 Behave in an offensive manner; or
18.7.4 Be guilty of misconduct not otherwise covered by the Laws of Badminton. ("International Badminton Federation").

With minor revisions to the language of interfering with the shuttle, the "Continuous Play, Misconduct, and Penalties" section remains in the Laws of Badminton today. This section's development illustrates the progressive addition of regulatory and auxiliary rules in a specific sport, and the current BWF Handbook is over 200 pages long ("Statutes BWF Corporate").

In the mid- and late-twentieth century, capitalism and consumer culture became progressively important relations within the assemblage of sport, functioning to connect elements of international, elite, and professional practices, activities, and events and their associated ecologies to one another, and these relations intersected with sporting policy and the ideology of fair play, as constitutive and regulatory rules were not always sufficient for governing athletes' comportment. This posed a problem for sporting organizations and IFs, as athlete comportment, and the circulation of media about athlete comportment could negatively affect revenue streams or public perception of an organization. As a result, IFs borrowed a policy tool from the field of business and began creating and implementing codes of conduct. According to Kapstein and Schwartz, a code of conduct, sometimes called an "ethical code" or a "code of ethics," can be defined as:

> a distinct and formal document containing a set of prescriptions developed by and for a company to guide present and future behaviour on multiple issues for at least its managers and employees toward one another, the company, external stakeholders, and/or society in general. (113)

Codes of conduct may be "general" in the sense of containing general precepts to guide conduct, or "specific" in the sense of identifying specific practices covered by the code, or they may include both general and specific elements. For sport organizations, code of conduct documents fill two important functions. First, the combination of specific and general guidelines in a code of conduct document concretizes the general principles of fair play, and, as such, provides a more robust mechanism for organizations to impose disciplinary action. Second, unlike regulatory rules which address in-competition behaviours, code of conduct documents also addresses pre-competition and post-competition behaviours. This allows sport organizations to guide, and often outright control, how athletes interact with multiple stakeholders, including spectators, sponsors, and the media.

The BWF code of conduct lists general principles such as "inappropriate conduct," regulations regarding post-competition behaviour such as "failure to fulfil media obligations," and, interestingly, regulatory rules, which address in-competition behaviour such as "trying to influence line judges" (*Laws of Badminton*). The code of conduct is significant as it extends the BWF's authority beyond any specific match. Additionally, the document's combination of specific and general principles, such as clause 4.16, which does not specify what kind of conduct is "clearly abusive or detrimental to the sport" (*Laws of Badminton*), gives the BWF an interpretative ability that allows them to engage with these principles in specific circumstances and apply them as they see fit. For players, however, the code of conduct plays a significant role in patterning behaviour during BWF-sanctioned competitions, as players must not only perform areas of specialized practice, they must also execute skills alongside vaguely articulated comportment edicts. In the case of the women's 2012 badminton scandal, the players were not disqualified for their badminton performance perse. Technically speaking, they did perform badminton skills such as serves and forehand swings. Instead, the players were disqualified because they failed to pattern their behaviour in relation to comportment shaped by the codified principles of fair play. This signals the significance of connective ideologies, like fair play, in the outcome of sporting activities and also suggests the complex matrices of factors that pattern the enactments of individual athletes during sport competitions.

Patriarchy and Gender in Match-Fixing for Sporting Reasons

The outcome of the 2012 women's pairs match-fixing scandal was noteworthy, in part, because of the harshness of the penalty. The incident marked the largest mass disqualification of athletes from different countries from a twenty-first-century Olympic Games for strategic match-fixing. It might be argued that the severity of penalty reflects twenty-first-century attitudes toward match-fixing, wherein organized international efforts to address match-fixing have been developed.[17] At the same time, however, it is striking that organizers were so quick to harshly condemn the players' actions, and it is difficult to ignore the role of gender or the history of the application of regulatory rules in women's sport.

Whether through the exclusion of women from sport or through the classification of athletes into male and female categories, most twenty-first-century elite, competitive, and professional sports divide competitors based on gender. The segregation of male and female athletes has been strongly influenced by the ideology of fair play and the unfair advantage discourse, "the persistent assumption that all males (born or 'made') have a physical advantage over all females (born or 'made')" (Sullivan 402). Because of this assumption, sport organizations frequently argue that it would be unfair for men and women to compete against one another. Alongside culturally held beliefs about the role of women in western countries, the unfair advantage discourse influenced the creation and implementation of auxiliary and regulatory rules in international women's sports throughout the twentieth and twenty-first centuries.[18] Such rules police dress code and uniform regulations and minimum age regulations; however, the most glaring example of the disproportionate application of auxiliary rules to women's bodies remains gender verification. Because of mandatory gender testing at the Olympics from 1967 to 1999, thousands of female athletes underwent compulsory gender verification in the twentieth century. While the Olympics officially discontinued the policy in 1999, case-by-case verification continued into the early twenty-first century.

In the 2010s, "female hyperandrogenism" policies replaced "gender verification" practices: however, as the title of the new policies suggests, concerns about hyperandrogenism do not apply to male athletes. Indeed, no male athlete has ever been subject to gender verification testing at the Olympics. Regardless of the name, these policies not only function to regulate women's bodies they also reify constructions of gender norms and sexual differences. As Vanessa Heggie notes,

> What the sex test effectively does, therefore, is provide an upper limit for women's sporting performance; there is a point at which your masculine-style body is declared "too masculine", and you are disqualified, regardless of your personal gender identity. For men there is no equivalent upper physiological limit – no kind of genetic, or hormonal, or physiological advantage is tested for, even if these would give a "super masculine" athlete a distinct advantage over the merely very athletic "normal" man. (158)

In the early twenty-first century, such policies have disproportionately affected athletes of colour and athletes from non-western countries. South African runner Caster Semenya is the most high-profile of these cases. In 2009, Semenya won the IAAF World Track Championships; following her win, it was leaked to the press that she would undergo gender verification testing (Padawar). Following the controversy, South Africa filed a human rights complaint with the United Nations, claiming the process was "sexist and racist" (qtd. in Padawar). Months later, it was announced that Semenya would keep her gold medal. Since 2009, Semenya has won several championships, including two gold medals in the women's 800-metre competition at the 2012 and 2016 Summer Olympic Games. Throughout her career, Semenya's participation has consistently been a point of controversy and legal battle. From 2018 through to 2021, Semenya challenged IAAF policies that required her (and other athletes with certain differences in sex development and androgen sensitivity) to take medication to lower their testosterone levels by taking her case to the Court of Arbitration of Sports, the Federal Supreme Court of Switzerland, and the European Court of Human Rights (Spary). Ultimately, she lost all three challenges/cases. Such cases demonstrate why examining the creation and application of regulatory and auxiliary rules is critical for understanding the full range of the effects of such rules in the domain of sport.

Unlike gender verification policies, codes of conduct are not gender specific. However, the language of the codes may allow for their uneven interpretation and application. In the case of the 2012 incident, without parameters for what using one's best efforts looks like or what kind of conduct qualifies as unsportsmanlike, the BWF officials retained the freedom to subjectively interpret the code. This is particularly troubling for female athletes. Studies show that regulatory rules in sports are more likely to be applied to female athletes than to male athletes (Souchon et al.). Moreover, the language of the BWF code—which has uncomfortable resonances with the vague language of gender verification policy documents of the early 2000s that did not specify the specific criteria for a challenge to an athlete's gender (IAAF)—opened the space for gender bias in its application. It is also hard to overlook the fact that all four teams represented non-western nations. Compared to summer sports like soccer, athletics, and swimming, badminton is a low-profile sport in western countries, and western commentators and official spokespersons were particularly harsh on the badminton players. For example, in an interview with BBC Radio 5, Gail Emms, a retired British badminton player, argued, "You cannot do this in an Olympic Games, this is something that is not acceptable" ("Badminton Players Disqualified") Further to this, David Mercer from the BBC called the athletes' actions "unforgivable," while Chairman of the London Olympic Organising Committee, Lord Coe, called the incident "depressing" ("Olympic badminton match-throwing depression"). Yet, not using one's best efforts in qualifying rounds is common practice in other sports. In track and field and swimming, for example, top swimmers and runners frequently conserve energy in heats. To this end, when the most decorated American swimmer of all time—Michael Phelps—saved energy in the heats of events across his multi-Olympic tenure, no IOC officials labelled his actions as "depressing" or "unforgivable." It is, in fact, difficult to imagine Olympic organizers criticizing any of its star western male athletes in this way.

Is it possible to definitively conclude that gender or nationality played a major role in the 2012 badminton incident? It is not. The BWF could have implemented the code of conduct to discipline male athletes had a scandal arisen in the men's tournament. And, it must be noted, that the athletes likely did not use "their best efforts," which was in direct violation of the code. However, given the history of the regulation of women's bodies in sport and the uneven application of auxiliary rules to female athletes as compared to their male counterparts, the gender of the athletes should not be ignored when examining the incident. No male athlete has been disqualified from an Olympic Games in the twenty-first century for strategic match-fixing, and it matters that during the world's largest and most prestigious multi-sport event, female athletes from the southern and eastern hemisphere countries received the most severe punishment possible. The incident also concretizes the intermingle between the meaningful relations in the performance genre of sport and actual sport performances wherein currents both reify the existence of the assemblage and also inflect the enactments and outcomes of contemporary performances.

Notes

1 The case study of this chapter is republished with permission. Copyright (2018) "The 2012 Olympic Badminton Scandal: Match-Fixing, Code of Conduct Documents, and Women's Sport," from The International Journal of Sport History by Kelsey Blair. Reproduced by permission of Taylor and Francis Group, LLC, a division of Informa plc.
2 The description is based on official video of the event. See: "Women's Doubles."
3 For theories of form in performance studies, see: MacAloon; Schechner; Singer; Turner.
4 For a discussion of the overlap and disconnections between the words—*assemblage* and *agencement,* see: Nail, 21.
5 For more on the character of assemblages, see: Deleuze, Gilles and Felix Guattari, 1–4; 330–60.
6 For more on these topics, see: Carrington; Hargreaves; Eitzen and Sage; Elias; Guttman; Dunning et al.; Ries
7 For more on the history of sport, see: Eitzen and Sage; Elias; Guttman; Ries.
8 For more on the histories of these sports, see: "History of the Law of the Game;" "History of Polo;" Naismith.
9 See: Norbert.
10 For more on the history of lacrosse, see: Cosentino; Robidoux.
11 See: "History of the Law of the Game;" "History of Polo."
12 See: Bateman; Holt; Malcolm.
13 See: Hall *Feminist;* Hall *The Girl and the Game;* Hargreaves *Sporting Females;* Hargreaves and Anderson; Messner *Power Play;* Messner and Sabo.
14 Ibid.
15 For more on the history of fair play, see: McIntosh Sherriden; Vamplew.
16 Ibid.
17 For more on efforts to intervene in twenty-first match-fixing, see: "Declarations on Core Principles of Sport Integrity."
18 For more on the history of gender- and sex-related policiejs in sport, see: Heggie; Sullivan.

References

"Athletics, N." *OED Online.* Oxford University Press, December, 2018, www.oed.com/view/Entry/12495.

Alleyne, Richard. *London 2012 Olympics: Badminton Players Charged with Misconduct after Appearing to Try to Lose Their Games.* August 1, 2012. *www.telegraph.co.uk*, http://www.telegraph.co.uk/sport/olympics/news/9443122/London-2012-Olympics-Badminton-players-charged-with-misconduct-after-appearing-to-try-to-lose-their-games.html.

American Badminton Association. *Official Rules American Badminton Association.* 1962, http://www.worldbadminton.com/rules/documents/ABALaws1962.pdf.

——— American Badminton Association. Official Rules, 1972, https://www.worldbadminton.com/rules/documents/ABALaws1972.pdf.

———. American Badminton Association. *The Official Rules,* 1966, https://www.worldbadminton.com/rules/documents/ABALaws1966.pdf.

Badminton Association of England. *The Laws of Badminton, as Revised in the Year 1939 and Adopted by the International Badminton Federation, Subsequently Revised 1949,* 1952.

Bawarshi, Anis S. and Mary Jo Reiff. *Genre: An Introduction to History, Theory, Research, and Pedagogy.* Parlor Press, 2010.

"Badminton Women's Doubles – Korea vs China | London 2012 Olympics," Olympics, July 31, 2012, https://www.youtube.com/watch?v=7mq1ioqiWEo.

Bateman, Anthony. *Cricket, Literature and Culture: Symbolising the Nation, Destabilising Empire.* Ashgate Pub, 2009, doi:10.4324/9781315574769.

Brownell, Susan. *The 1904 Anthropology Days and Olympic Games: Sport, Race, and American Imperialism.* University of Nebraska Press, 2008.

———. "Wushu and the Olympic Games. Combination of East and West, or Class of Body Cultures." *Perfect Bodies: Sports, Medicine and Immortality: Ancient and Modern*, edited by Vivienne Lo, vol. 188; no. 188, British Museum, 2012, pp. 59–69.

Carrington, Ben. *Race, Sport and Politics: The Sporting Black Diaspora.* Sage Pub, 2010.

Clarey, Christopher. "Figure Skating: 2 French Officials Suspended 3 Years in Skating Scandal." *The New York Times,* May 2002, http://www.nytimes.com/2002/05/01/sports/figure-skating-2-french-officials-suspended-3-years-in-skating-scandal.html. Accessed 26 June 2017.

Conquergood, Dwight. "Cultural Struggles." *Rethinking Ethnography: Towards a Critical Cultural Politics,* Ann Arbor: University of Michigan Press, 2013, pp. 81–103.

Cosentino, Frank. "Afros, Aboriginals and Amateur Sport in Pre-World War One Canada." Ottawa, *Canadian Historical Association,* 1988.

Curry, Graham and Eric Dunning. "The Folk Antecedents of Modern Football." *Association Football: A Study in Figurational Sociology,* Routledge, Taylor & Francis Group, 2015, doi:10.4324/9781315738369.

Sport Integrity Global Alliance. "Declaration on Core Principles of Sport Integrity." Siga-sport, 2016, https://siga-sport.com/declaration-of-core-principles-on-sport-integrity/.

"Olympic Badminton Match-Throwing Depressing, Says Coe – Video." *The Guardian,* https://www.theguardian.com/sport/video/2012/aug/01/olympic-badminton-match-throwing-coe-video. Accessed 25 June 2017.

Dunning, Eric, et al. *Sport Histories: Figurational Studies in the Development of Modern Sports.* Routledge, 2004, doi:10.4324/9780203497432.

Deleuze, Gilles and Felix Guattari. *A Thousand Plateaus: Capitalism and Schizophrenia Translation and Foreword by Brian Massumi.* Minneapolis: University of Minnesota Press, 1987.

Eitzen, D. Stanley and George Harvey Sage. *Sociology of North American Sport.* 7th ed., McGraw-Hill, 2003.

Elias, Norbert. "The Genesis of Sport as a Sociological Problem." *The Sociology of Sport: Selected Readings,* edited by Eric Dunning, London, 1971.

Federation International de Football Association. *Laws of the Game 2013/2014.* Federation International de Football Association, 2013.

Guttman, Allen. *Games and Empires: Modern Sports and Cultural Imperialism.* New York: Columbia University Press, 1994.

Hall, Ann. *The Girl and the Game: A History of Women's Sport in Canada.* Second edition, University of Toronto Press, 2016.

———. *Immodest & Sensational: 150 Years of Canadian Women in Sport.* James Lorimer & Company, 2008.

———. *Sport and Gender: A Feminist Perspective on the Sociology of Sport.* University of Calgary, 1978.

Hargreaves, Jennifer, ed. *Sport, Culture, and Ideology*. Routledge, 1982.
———. *Sporting Females: Critical Issues in the History and Sociology of Women's Sport*. Routledge, 2002. www-taylorfrancis-com.ezproxy.library.ubc.ca, doi:10.4324/9780203221945.
Hargreaves, Jennifer and Eric Anderson. *Routledge Handbook of Sport, Gender and Sexuality*. Routledge, 2014.
Hargreaves, Jennifer and Patricia Anne Vertinsky, editors. *Physical Culture, Power, and the Body*. Routledge, 2007.
Holt, Richard. "Cricket and Englishness: The Batsman as Hero." *International Journal of Sport History*, vol. 13, no. 1, 1996, pp. 48–70.
"History of the Laws of the Game – From 1863 to the Present Day." *FIFA.com*, http://www.fifa.com/about-fifa/who-we-are/the-laws/index.html.
"History of Polo | Polo Museum." *Polo Museum*, http://www.polomuseum.com/sport-polo/history-polo.
"History of the LAWS of Badminton." *World Badminton*, http://www.worldbadminton.com/rules/history.htm.
International Association of Athletics Federations Medical and Anti-Doping Commission 2006. *The IAAF Policy on Gender Verification*. Monte Carlo: IAAF, 2006.
International Association of Athletics Federations Medical and Anti-Doping Commission. IAAF Policy on Gender Verification. Monte Carlo: IAAF, 2000.
International Badminton Federation. "*The Laws of Badminton. As Amended and Adopted by the IBF through May*," 1992.
International Olympic Committee. "The International Olympic Committee and the Modern Olympic Games," https://www.olympic.org/olympic-studies-centre/collections/official-publications/olympic-charters.
Muel, Kaptein and Mark S. Schwartz. "The Effectiveness of Business Codes: A Critical Examination of Existing Studies and the Development of an Integrated Research Model," *Journal of Business Ethics, vol.* 77, no. 2, 2008, p. 113.
Laws of Badminton, BWF Badminton, May 22, 2022, https://corporate.bwfbadminton.com/statutes/#1513733461252-a16ae05d-1fc9.
Levine, Caroline. *Forms: Whole, Rhythm, Hierarchy, Network*. STU-Student, Princeton University Press, 2015.
Malcolm, Dominic. *Globalizing Cricket: Englishness, Empire and Identity*. Bloomsbury Academic, 2013.
"Badminton Players Disqualified for Trying to Lose." *ESPN.Com*, 1 Aug. 2012, http://www.espn.com/olympics/summer/2012/badminton/story/_/id/8221408/2012-london-olympics-eight-badminton-players-disqualified-trying-lose-matches.
Heggie, Vanessa. "Testing Sex and Gender in Sports; Reinventing, Reimagining and Reconstructing Histories." *Endeavour*, vol. 34, no. 4, 2010, pp. 157–63, doi:10.1016/j.endeavour.2010.09.005.
Messner, Michael A. *Out of Play: Critical Essays on Gender and Sport*. State University of New York Press, 2007.
Messner, Michael A. and Donald F. Sabo. *Sport, Men, and the Gender Order: Critical Feminist Perspectives*. Human Kinetics Books, 1990.
Nail, Thomas. "What Is an Assemblage?" *Substance*, vol. 46, no. 1, 2017, pp. 21–37.
Owen, Stephen. "Special Topic: Remapping Genre – Genres in Motion." *Publications of the Modern Language Association of America*, vol. 122, no. 5, 2007, p. 1389.
Riess, Steven A. *Sport in Industrial America, 1850–1920*. Harlan Davidson, 1995.

Robidoux, Michael A. "Imagining a Canadian Identity through Sport: A Historical Interpretation of Lacrosse and Hockey." *The Journal of American Folklore*, vol. 115, no. 456, 2002, pp. 209–25, doi:10.1353/jaf.2002.0021.

Shipley, Amy. "Ryan Lochte, Michael Phelps set for showdown after 400 IM prelims," *Washington Post*, June 25, 2012, https://www.washingtonpost.com/sports/olympics/ryan-lochte-michael-phelps-set-for-showdown-after-400-im-prelims/2012/06/25/gJQAZ96A2V_story.html.

Singer, Milton B. *Man's Glassy Essence: Explorations in Semiotic Anthropology*. Indiana University Press, 1984.

Souchon, Nicolas, et al. "Referees' Decision Making about Transgressions: The Influence of Player Gender at the Highest National Level." *Psychology of Women Quarterly*, vol. 33, no. 4, March, 2009, pp. 445–52. *SAGE Journals*, doi:10.1111/j.1471-6402.2009.01522.x.

Turner, Victor. "Liminal to Liminoid, in Play, Flow, and Ritual: An Essay in Comparative Symbology." *Ce Institute Pamphlet – Rice University Studies*, vol. 60, no. 3, 1974, pp. 53–94.

MacAloon, John J., et al., editors. *Rite, Drama, Festival, Spectacle: Rehearsals toward a Theory of Cultural Performance*. Institute for the Study of Human Issues, 1984.

McIntosh, Peter C. *Fair Play: Ethics in Sport and Education*. Heinemann, 1979.

Padawar, Ruth. "The Humiliating Practice of Sex-Testing Female Athletes," *New York Time*, June 28, 2016, https://www.nytimes.com/2016/07/03/magazine/the-humiliating-practice-of-sex-testing-female-athletes.html.

Schechner, Richard. *Performance Theory*. Routledge, 2004, doi:10.4324/9780203426630.

Sheridan, Heather. "Conceptualizing 'Fair Play': A Review of the Literature." *European Physical Education Review*, vol. 9, no. 2, 2003, pp. 163–84, doi:10.1177/1356336X03009002003.

Sullivan, Claire F. "Gender Verification and Gender Policies in Elite Sport: Eligibility and 'Fair Play.'" *Journal of Sport & Social Issues*, vol. 35, no. 4, 2011, pp. 400–19, doi:10.1177/0193723511426293.

Spary, Sara. "Caster Semenya Appears to European Human Rights over 'discriminatory' testosterone limit." *CNN Sports*, February 26, 2021, https://www.cnn.com/2021/02/26/sport/caster-semenya-appeal-scli-intl-spt/index.html.

Vamplew, Wray. "Playing with the Rules: Influences on the Development of Regulation in Sport." *The International Journal of the History of Sport*, vol. 24, no. 7, 2007, pp. 843–71, 10.1080/09523360701311745.

Walker, Peter and Haroon Siddique. "Eight Olympic Badminton Players Disqualified for 'Throwing Game.'" *The Guardian*, August 1, 2012, https://www.theguardian.com/sport/2012/aug/01/london-2012-badminton-disqualified-olympics. Accessed 3 February 2018.

Zaksaite, Salomeja. "Match-Fixing: The Shifting Interplay between Tactics, Disciplinary Offence and Crime." *The International Sports Law Journal*, vol. 13, no. 3, 2013, pp. 287–93, doi:10.1007/s40318-013-0031-3.

2
CONFIGURATIONS AND FORMATIONS

The Patterning of Behaviour in Performance Activities

In 1899, Nora Cleary, a teacher at Ontario's Windsor Collegiate Institute, read the rules of basketball from a booklet produced by the Spalding Company to a group of female students (Hall *Girl* 31). Following her reading, the girls attempted to play a basketball game. This marks the first known instance of women's basketball in Canada (Hall *Girl* 31). One hundred years later, a group of teenage girls gather in a gymnasium in North Vancouver, British Columbia. Teammates are grouped into pairs, one offensive player, and one defensive player. Spread around the half-court of a high school gymnasium, the offensive players hold basketballs with two hands. They practice moving the ball from one side of their body to another while the defensive player attempts to disrupt their movements or bat the ball away. I am one of the players in the second scene. These two basketball performances—separated by a century—are connected to one another by my writing (which ties an explicit thread between them) and also by the genealogy of basketball practice in Canada.

In the previous chapter, I took a broader approach to sport performances and theorized the meaningful sets of relations between activities in the performance genre of sport. In this chapter, I narrow the scope of my analysis and focus on the patterning of behaviour for athletes in specific sports. To do so, I introduce two new critical terms: configuration, which queries the stitching together of interpersonal behaviours and sequences of action; and formation, which attends to the patterning of individual behaviours. In applying these terms to the case of women's basketball, I aim to demonstrate how they facilitate a rigorous analysis of the physical, psychological, and philosophical effects of the patterning of behaviour in sport performances. More specifically, I examine one of the core principles of twenty-first-century basketball practice: the vertical cylinder, or the concept that every basketball player has

DOI: 10.4324/9781003275879-3

a right to the space of an imaginary cylinder that extends around her shoulders, above her head, and below her feet. Tracing the emergence of the concept of the vertical cylinder from the twentieth century to the present, I aim to illuminate the important, but often overlooked, role women have played in the game's development and to illustrate the physical, psychological, and philosophical effects of the vertical cylinder principle for twenty-first-century women's basketball players.

Configurations: Shaping Performance Activities

"Structure" sometimes gets a bad name in the Humanities, as it can connote something that is rigid, prescriptive, or universal. As Victor Turner suggests in his forward to *A Ritual Process,* "We have been to prone to think, in static terms, that cultural superstructures are passive mirrors, mere reflections of substructural productive modes and relations or of the political processes that enforce the dominance of the productively privileged" (vii). "Structure," the way I am using the term here, is not static or universal. A structure does not *determine* an outcome; it can be followed, reversed, parodied, disrupted, subverted. Structures do, however, stitch together movements and behaviours—from the minutia of an eye flick during a circus performance to the broad orientation of a group of football players—in recognizable and repeatable ways, which perhaps requires an even more nuanced term. A key word that gained prominence in a range of fields in the humanities and social sciences in the 1970s, frame is one of the more popular and potentially generative words for thinking about the structures of activities across performance genres. Erving Goffman argued that frames are "the principles of organization which govern events" (10) and proposed an extended theory for frame analysis.[1] Performance studies scholars such as Richard Schechner, Diana Taylor, and John MacAloon have used the term frame to analyze performance structures.[2] Critically, however, the term "frame" is not without its problems. For starters, frame can be a rigid and prescriptive metaphor for thinking about actual life. The analogy of a picture frame implies a fixed boundary that is outside the bodies of participants within the frame. Life, as experienced by actual individuals, is not so simple. Does the theatre performance begin when the curtain goes up? When the spectator walks into the auditorium? When the actor enters the green room? When the house manager opens the building? Who gets to do the framing? The participants? An outside observer? Moreover, theoretical usage of the term gets complicated because in a performance event there can be layers upon layers of frames, a phenomenon that Goffman calls lamination. Indeed, while frames are useful for identifying general principles of organization, they are less well-suited for honing-in on the details of how these principles manifest in concrete instances of performance or for examining the effects of the relations between principles for the patterning of behaviour.

According to the *Oxford English Dictionary*, configuration refers to "arrangement of parts or elements in a particular form or figure; the form, shape, figure, resulting from such arrangement" ("Configuration, n"). Drawing from this definition, I use "configuration" to refer to the rules, laws, traditions, and conventions that stitch together sequences of behaviour into activities. Of course, some configurations will be comprised of more than one of these elements than others. Basketball, for example, is comprised of more rules and laws than conventions and Bhangra dance is comprised of more conventions and traditions than rules. The elements of an activity's configuration provide the concrete details of a performance's abstract qualities: specifications about space, time, objects, and the sequencing of behaviours and blocks of action. Configurations are, in a sense, like the pieces of a toy set; different configurations may share some pieces, but each configuration will have its own unique shape. Synchronized swimming and diving both sequence action so that it takes place in a pool but their configurations organize the space within the pool differently. Importantly, like other key concepts that help conceptualize the underpinnings of human behaviours, such as Robin Bernstein's "scriptive things" and Pierre Bourdieu's "habitus," configurations are not outside of bodies; bodies enact them.[3] Take, for example, the segmentation of space. Whether it be a stage's edge or the lines of a playing field, the segmentation of space may be outside the individual in the sense that the borders exist in physical space. However, these borders only matter if people recognize them by patterning their behaviour in accordance with them. In sports, this often means respecting the boundaries of the playing space. In avant-garde western theatre, this might mean actively breaking the boundaries of the playing space. A configuration shapes what is likely (or is supposed to) happen in a performance. What actually takes place, however, is a completely different matter.

To rigorously analyze configurations, a further distinction is useful. There are two kinds of configurations: general and located. An activity's general configuration refers to the sequencing of behaviour structured by a combination of laws, conventions, rules, and traditions that make the activity recognizable *as* the activity across time and space. To borrow a term from philosophy, the general configuration gives an activity its quiddity, its "itness." An activity's located configuration, on the other hand, refers to the sequencing of behaviour structured by the conventions, laws, rules, and traditions located in time and bound to a specific place. In sports, located activity configurations are typically determined by leagues, organizations, and federations such as the National Basketball Association (NBA) in the United States or the International Basketball Federation (FIBA), both of which determine a specific set of rules for their respective leagues. In theatre, dance, and music, a located activity configuration typically emerges from the communities in which performances take place. It is the distinction between the broad conventions of traditional western theatre performances in Canada and the

TABLE 2.1 NBA vs. FIBA Configurations

Rule	NBA	FIBA
Overall length of game	48 minutes	40 minutes
Length of quarters	12 minutes	10 minutes
Arc radius of 3 point line	23 feet 9 inches (7.24 meters)	22 feet 2 inches (6.75 meters)
Number of personal fouls allowed per player	6	5

United States and attending a production of *Macbeth* at Vancouver's Bard on the Beach festival in 2018 in Vancouver, British Columbia. To further explain the concept of configuration, I turn to an examination of the emergence of the general configuration of basketball.

The General Configuration of Basketball and the Emergence of Women's Basketball

In the field of design, the term "affordance" is used to describe the potentials and constraints of materials, environments, and objects—both physical and digital. Wood affords solidity. Copper affords conduction. An elevator button affords pushing. A kitchen chair affords sitting. Designed phenomena can have intentional or anticipated affordances as well as unintentional or unexpected affordances. I can use a chair as intended and sit on it, or I might stand on a chair to change a light bulb or use the back of a chair as a clothes' rack. Regardless how creative or imaginative the user, however, materials, objects, and environments have both potentials and constraints. A kitchen chair constrains suppleness and flexibility and so I cannot use a kitchen chair as a blanket. While the term was not intended for application in performance studies, it offers a useful approach for conceptualizing the potentials and constraints of occasions. In the case of activities, a performance's affordances are shaped by configurations. To identify an activity's affordances, then, it is necessary to identify a configuration's key features. The general configuration of basketball offers an indicative example.

The key features of basketball first emerged in 1891 when Dr. James Naismith created an indoor game at a YMCA in Massachusetts. A year later, Dr. Naismith published thirteen rules that specified parameters for segmenting space and time and for stitching together behaviours and sequences of action during "basketball" games. These rules mark the emergence of the general configuration of basketball. Like most late nineteenth-century sporting activities, the number of rules expanded over the twentieth century, and the International Basketball Federation "Official Basketball Rules 2020" manual is one pages and includes eight broad rule categories such as "Playing

Court and equipment" (6) and "Playing Regulations" (18); each of these has several sub-articles, such as "equipment" (11) and "status of the ball" (18). Despite the proliferation and detail of the rules of basketball in the last one hundred years, the general principles of the game are similar. In basketball, two teams of individuals compete against one another to throw a ball through a hoop raised in the air. An individual cannot run with the basketball; instead, they must bounce—or "dribble," in basketball terms—the ball while moving. The performance is divided into sections. Some contact between individuals is permitted but tackling is not allowed; the game takes place on a court with boundaries that clearly demarcate the playing space. The knitting together of these key principles stitch together the conventional sequences of action of a basketball game. Take, for example, the division of a game into sections. In basketball, play is traditionally divided into two halves or four quarters. As such, basketball games are organized around extended sequences of action and shorter sequences of rest. Within the sequence of action, principles pertaining to the activity's objective, to the demarcation of space, and to behaviours combine to shape the general set of behaviours that are likely to take place wherein players behave within the court's boundaries, bounce the ball when they run, and attempt to throw (or "shoot" in basketball terms), the ball through the hoop. The combination of principles also shapes unlikely or unexpected enactments. In the early twenty-first century, for example, the principles of the general configuration of basketball mean that it is unlikely that basketball players will perform a choreographed song and dance number in the middle of the second quarter; it is equally unlikely that, during a Broadway musical theatre performance, one performer will push another performer toward the ground as the first is about to belt the high-note of the Act One finale (unless the pushing is part of the choreography). Of course, neither situation is impossible, but the configuration of basketball and musical theatre mean that some sequences of actions far more likely than others. In other words, an activity's configuration shapes its behavioural affordances, it's potentials and constraints as they pertain to enactment.

In addition to shaping a performance activity's affordances, configurations prompt matrices of orientations between bodies and objects. In basketball, for instance, the rules of the game prompt encounters between a player's body, other players' bodies, coaches' bodies, officials' bodies, the ball, the hoops, and potentially the spectators. By contrast, the configuration of theatre prompts encounters and orientations between a performer's body, other performers' bodies, props, set pieces, crew, and potentially the audience. In both cases, the configuration shapes the quality of these encounters by guiding orientations. In basketball, the objective of the game (to score more baskets than the other team), in combination with the segmentation of space into two halves, the position of the hoops on the court, and rules regarding how long players and/or the ball can remain in a particular location on the court, guide a continuous, dynamic, stream of large and micro-orientations between players, coaches, officials, the ball, and the hoops. The significance of these micro-orientations begins to be suggested by a close examination of players' relationships to the basketball.

The ball is an integral component of the configuration of basketball: the object of the game is to shoot the ball through the hoop; possession of the ball determines whether a team is on offence or defence; players cannot run with the ball unless they dribble; etc. Though the focus of affect theorist Brian Massumi's work is quite different from mine, his lengthy description of soccer in *Parables of the Virtual* helps illuminate the phenomenological dimensions of such regulations:

> The ball is the focus of every player, and the object of every gesture. Superficially, when a player kicks the ball, the player is the subject of the movement, and the ball is the object. But if by subject we mean the point of unfolding of a tendential movement, then it is clear that the player is not the subject of the play. The ball is .... Where and how it bounces differentially potentializes and depotentializes the entire field, intensifying and de-intensifying the exertions of the players and the movements of the team. The ball is the subject of the play. (73)

Like soccer, in basketball, the rules function to orient players, officials, and spectators in relation to the ball. Significantly, in a basketball game, orientation is not singular or static; one is constantly orienting oneself towards (or away from) the ball.

While it is undoubtedly possible to examine the agency of a ball in a sport contest, as Massumi does, what is most significant about the ball in basketball for my analysis is not its subjecthood but the consequences of repeated orientations. In *Queer Phenomenology*, Sara Ahmed argues that bodies "acquire orientation through the repetitions of some actions over others, as actions that have certain 'objects' in view, whether they are physical objects required to do the work (the writing table, the pen, the keyboard) or the ideal objects that one identifies with" (58); she further suggests that in the repetition of actions, we orient "ourselves toward some objects more than others, including not only physical objects (the different kinds of tables) but also objects of thought, feeling, and judgment, as well as objects in the sense of aims, aspirations, and objectives" (56). In basketball, by repeatedly directing one's body toward or away from the ball, a relation between body and ball is formed. One of the dimensions of this relation is material. A basketball is approximately 500 grams in weight, with a diameter of approximately 24 centimetres, and is constructed of leather or rubber. To put this in relation to my own body, it is big enough that I cannot easily hold it with one hand, harder than my flesh but suppler than copper, and light enough that I can easily carry it in a bag alongside a pair of shoes. The ball's materiality inflects my encounter with it: its weight in combination with its size prompts me to hold it with two hands; it is heavy and hard enough that if it hits me in the face, I will experience pain.

A controversy involving a change in the material of NBA basketballs in 2006 offers an indicative instance of the intensities, imaginations, and investments potentially prompted by a player's encounter with the ball. In 2006, the NBA introduced a microfiber composite ball. The ball, ever-so-creatively dubbed the "New Ball," was intended to replace the traditional leather basketball. By 2006, many American high schools and colleges were already using the New Ball, a ball that was cheaper to produce and, by consequence, cheaper to purchase. NBA's primary ball manufacturer, Spalding, sent a New Ball to every NBA player in the summer of 2006 so that players could adjust to the new material before the beginning of regular season in the fall. However, the introduction of the ball did not go as the league hoped, and the backlash against the change in ball material was instant. A quotation from star player Ray Allen captures the players' general attitude toward the New Ball. He said, "It's changed a lot of what we are and who we are" (Gaine). He went on to note, "At the beginning of the year, I kept an open mind to it. Overall, you see the league, shots aren't like they used to be. Every player I've talked to is in disagreement with the ball" (Gaine). The intensity of the player's response to the ball culminated in a complaint filed by the NBA Players' Association to the National Labor Relations Board in December of 2006. On December 11th of that year, the NBA officially surrendered to the players' demands, and in a statement, the NBA argued, "Although testing performed by Spalding and the NBA demonstrated that the new composite basketball was more consistent than leather, and statistically there has been an improvement in shooting, scoring, and ball-related turnovers, the most important statistic is the view of our players" (Gaine).

Carefully crafted not to undermine Spalding's merchandise, the statement at once acquiesced to the players' demands and undermined their response. The NBA, perhaps unsurprisingly, took little responsibility for the uproar. What the league should have guessed, however, was that players were bound to have an intense response to a significant change to the ball. After all, the texture, weight, appearance, and smell of a leather ball are an essential component of the sensory dimension of participating in a basketball game, and for elite basketball players, the ball is an object a player encounters, orients themselves toward, and handles repeatedly. As Ahmed argues:

> To be orientated is also to be turned toward certain objects, those that help us to find our way. These are the objects we recognize, so that when we face them we know which way we are facing. They might be landmarks or other familiar signs that give us our anchoring points. (*Queer* 1)

She goes on to suggest that "the familiar is shaped by actions that reach out toward objects that are already within reach" and, as such, to be "orientated is also to extend the reach of the body" (*Queer* 7). Within the context of a basketball game, the materiality of the ball is an anchoring point for sensational familiarity, and the sensations prompted by the materiality of the ball are associated with the ability of a player to extend the reach of his or her body into space. Given this, of course the players were invested in the ball's materiality. As becomes evident from an examination of the located configuration of women's basketball, however, the relations prompted by the general configuration of basketball are cross-cut by specific articulations of located configurations and a range of social, cultural, and political factors.

The Located Activity Configuration of Modified Women's Basketball in the United States

Women's basketball in the United States in the late nineteenth and early twentieth centuries offers an important example of the relationship between general and located configurations.[4] Women began playing basketball as early as 1892. Significantly, however, the trajectory of the early history of the configuration of women's basketball was markedly different from that of men's basketball. As has been outlined by feminist sport historians such as Ann Hall, Patricia Vertinsky, and Nancy Cole Dosch, by the mid-nineteenth century, the medical profession played a key role in controlling and regulating women's bodies. As Cole Dosch argues, "The male medical conception of women's physiology and sexuality reinforced a conservative view of women's social and domestic roles" (125) and "using a mixture of evolutionary theory and societal stereotypes, physicians explained and reinforced notions of female form and frailty" (126) in relation to white, upper and middle class, women. Such attitudes regarding women's health and bodies influenced the development of women's basketball, and, as is evident from the sex and gender verification policies in contemporary sport examined in chapter one, such attitudes continue to influence women's sporting practices.

The regulations regarding physical contact have always been central to the general activity configuration of basketball. In fact, James Naismith was inspired to invent basketball because he wanted a game for his students that was suitable for an indoor gymnasium and that was not too rough. One of the thirteen original rules specifically addressed physical contact. The rule read, "No shouldering, holding, pushing, tripping, or striking in any way an opponent shall be allowed" ("Naismith's Rules'). Performing any of these actions resulted in a foul, and from the 1890s to the early 1920s, the specifications regarding specific fouls increased and the severity of the language addressing roughness strengthened. Unsurprisingly, roughness was a significant concern for women's participation in basketball. Basketball was considered too vigorous, quick, and physical for women in the United States. Influenced by widespread cultural beliefs regarding women's health, psychology, and comportment, American educators, such as Senda Berenson and Clara Gregory, felt it necessary to modify the rules of basketball for female participants. In the first official publication of Berenson's rules by Spalding, Berenson cautioned that without careful supervision and adjustments, basketball could have a negative effect for female participants (Berenson 31–45). She argued, "Rough and vicious play seems worse in women than in men. A certain amount of roughness is deemed necessary to bring out manliness in our young men. Surely rough play can have no possible excuse in our young women" (Berenson 23–24). She then went on to suggest that "unless a game as exciting as basketball is carefully guided by such rules as will eliminate roughness, the great desire to win and the excitement of the game will make our women do sadly unwomanly things" (Berenson 37).

Significantly, one of the key differences between the configurations of women's and men's basketball pertained to physical contact and the principle of the vertical plane, a concept that is integral to the configuration and formation of basketball in the twenty-first century. In the first official publication of Berenson's rules, she added a regulation that addressed physical contact between players. She banned "snatching or batting [the] ball from hands of an opponent" (Berenson 84) and decreed that "no guarding may be done over the opponent's person when she has the ball" (Berenson 83). By 1908, the wording of the latter rule was re-articulated as "overguarding," which was defined as "guarding with one or both hands or arms or body not in the vertical plane" (Davenport 94). In other words, players could not touch other players or enter another player's air space.

In the early twentieth century, the vertical plane rule meant that the formation for players who used the modified rules differed sharply from those who did not. Images from the *1905 Basket Ball Guide for Women* help illuminate this difference. In the first two images, players break the modified rules. In these images, the defensive player can cross the threshold of the vertical plane and can snatch the ball out of the offensive player's hands; the offensive player, then, has to hold the ball and/or pivot away from the pressure in order to make her next move. In the third image, the players enact the modified rules, and the defensive player is not permitted to cross into the offensive player's physical space. Consequently, the offensive player does not have to protect her space. Instead, she focuses on court vision, the ability to see her teammates and the hoop, and the execution of the next skill. As players catch and defend the ball repeatedly throughout the course of a basketball game, this seemingly minor rule significantly impacted the formation of modified rules for women's basketball. It was so significant, in fact, that it led to the modification of the performance

52 Configurations and Formations

FIGURE 2.1 AND 2.2 An Example of "Wrong Guarding" from Basketball for Women (1905).

configuration of women's basketball as a whole. As Joanna Davenport argues, because of the vertical plane rule, "there was no way to defend against a two-handed overhead throw" (88), and as such, players who perfected the two-hand shot were virtually impossible to stop. Rather than changing the vertical plane rule, in 1921, the scoring system was adjusted so that two-hand overhead shots were only worth one point instead of the usual two points (Davenport 88). From 1901 to 1931, the modified rules meant that modified

FIGURE 2.3 An Example of "Right Guarding" from Basketball for Women (1905)

women's basketball configuration in the United States differed markedly from the general configuration of basketball during this period.

A range of factors influenced shifts in the modified women's basketball configuration in the United States in the early twentieth century, including but not limited to women's suffrage, changes in women's physical education, increasing societal acceptance of women's participation in sports, the heightened popularity of club basketball for women, and the governance of women's sports.[5] Following this, in 1932, a key rule change was implemented in the American women's basketball configuration: the "overguarding" rule was eliminated and players were, finally, permitted to play defence on any plane. The period following this rule change was indicative of shifting attitudes toward physical contact in women's basketball. The 1934–35 rulebook stated:

> Although basketball is theoretically a 'no contact game,' it is obvious that personal contact cannot be avoided entirely when players are moving rapidly over a limited space. The personal contact resulting from such movement should not be penalized unless roughness has resulted.
> *("Basketball Official Playing Rules"* 14)

As Joanna Davenport argues, "This change had a dramatic effect on the game as it impacted both offensive and defensive play. Consequently, the game became more exciting and skillful, because now the offense had to learn to be more evasive and the defense player could truly play defense" (89). Over the next forty years, the modifications in the rules of women's basketball were slowly eliminated so that by the early 1970s, the located configuration of women's basketball closely resembled the located configuration of men's basketball in the United States.

Though the modified rules no longer officially exist, the residue of the anxiety about women's bodies remains embedded in the configuration of women's basketball. One example of this is the introduction of the size six basketball, which is one inch in circumference smaller than a size seven ball and is colloquially known as the "women's ball." The logic of the introduction of the women's ball was predicated on the logic described by Ahmed regarding the relationship between objects and bodies:

> Objects, as well as spaces, are made for some kinds of bodies more than others. Objects are made to size as well as made to order: while they come in a range of sizes, the sizes also presume certain kinds of bodies as having "sizes" that will "match." In this way, bodies and their objects tend toward each other; they are orientated toward each other, and are shaped by this orientation. When orientation "works," we are occupied. The failure of something to work is a matter of a failed orientation: a tool is used by a body for which it was not intended, or a body uses a tool that does not extend its capacity for action.
>
> (*Queer Phenomenology* 27)

In the case of women's basketball, however, this logic was underpinned by anxieties regarding the capacity of female bodies. Though there were isolated attempts to reduce the size of the ball in women's basketball in the 1930s and 1950s (Podmenik, Keskosek and Erculj 29), it was not until the 1970s that the idea gained any traction in the United States. This was, in large, part due to the efforts of basketball player Karen Logan. In her proposal to the governing body of women's collegiate athletics, she argued:

> Almost all sports, with the exception of basketball, vary the size, weight and nature of the equipment to compensate for the physical size and anatomical differences of women. These compensations are designed to insure equal mobility with the same rule structure of each sport. Thus, by not handicapping female athletes with oversized, misfit equipment, the quality of the product is preserved.
>
> (qtd. in Porter, 105)

The committee rejected Logan's proposal. A year later, however, Logan successfully pitched the idea to Bill Byrne, owner of the new formed Women's Basketball League (WBL). Unlike reaction to the "new ball" in the NBA in 2006, the materiality of the women's ball did not prompt widespread outrage in 1978. Rather, it prompted widespread uncertainty. According to interviews with players conducted by Karra Porter for her historical account of the WBL, there was a variety of responses to the ball. Kathy Solano, for example, reported that she loved the ball, saying "I'm a point guard, and at 5'6" I've got good-sized hands. I felt I could do a lot more with it" (qtd. in Porter, 108). Other players, however, disliked the ball. Marie Kocurek, for example, described the introduction of the ball as a "slap in the face" (qtd. in Porter, 108) to women's basketball players.

Over the next decade, the ball continued to generate uncertainty in the women's basketball community: How does ball size affect the enactment of specific skills? How does it affect style of play? Do women truly benefit from a smaller ball? Might the smaller ball facilitate dunking in women's basketball? If so, would dunking help spark increased interest in the women's game?[6] Despite contradictory evidence (Porter 110–5), however, the small ball was adopted for use in the NCAA in the 1984–1985 season, and when the WNBA was formed in 1999, it, too, mandated a smaller ball ("WNBA Official Rules"). FIBA was slower to adopt the ball for use in international basketball, but after decades of flip-flopping between the size six and seven balls, the smaller ball became the standard ball size in international women's basketball in 2004 (Podmenik; Leskosek; Erculj). Though the small ball is not directly linked to the original modified women's basketball rules, it is difficult not to see the regulation of a smaller ball for women as indicative of the spectres of anxiety regarding female bodies that remain embedded in the configuration of women's basketball. It is also difficult not to note that the size seven ball is often conceptualized as the standard ball size, illustrating how male bodies are frequently still the imagined ideal sporting body. This is not to say, however, that all elements of the women's basketball configuration function evenly across time. As a study of the vertical plane makes clear, the effects of the principles that underpin practice are malleable and mutable. To examine further, however, a term for studying the patterning of individual behaviour is needed.

The Structuring of Practice through Formation

Configurations provide the critical language to analyze the structuring of behaviours between bodies and objects during performance occasions; to understand the patterning of behaviour that takes place within individual bodies during performance occasions, however, a different critical term is needed. Performance studies scholars have frequently theorized the transmission of embodied knowledges. Richard Schechner uses the terms "twice-behaved behaviour" and "restored behaviour" to examine how human enactments become linked together[7]; Diana Taylor introduces the concept of the repertoire, which refers to a repository of embodied and gestural knowledge,[8] and Joseph Roach introduces the term *surrogation* to describe how culture re-creates and re-produces itself through performance.[9] But, there is not yet an approach that is specifically designed for examining the patterning of behaviour during cultural occasions or for investigating how, precisely, areas of technique and performance occasions intersect to pattern practice.

As noted in the introduction of this project, I follow Ben Spatz's distinction between technique and practice, wherein the former refers to embodied knowledge that is transmissible across time and space and the latter refers to concrete groupings of enactments. Technique plays a key role in patterning movements across genres of performance. The area of technique of ballet, for instance, patterns individual enactments in dance performances. Similarly, the area of technique of association football shapes behaviours in sporting matches but can also pattern behaviours in theatrical performances such as American stage play *The Wolves* (2016) or West End musical *Bend it Like Beckham: The Musical* (2015). As these examples suggest, some areas of technique share the same name as activities and practices (football match, football technique, football practice; ballet performance, ballet technique, ballet practice). It is important to remember, however, that these related phenomena are distinct from one another. Areas of technique can move across socio-cultural domains and performance genres: skills patterned by techniques from ballet might be incorporated into a circus performance and techniques from association football might be integrated into a theatre performance. And, in the same way that the lines of a field shape how a player moves in space during a game, the edge of a raised stage might influence an actor's behaviours. This begins to suggest an important facet for the patterning of behaviour in performance occasions: individual's enactments are not only shaped by areas of technique.

As part of his theorization on the relationship between areas of technique and practice, Ben Spatz argues that, alongside areas of technique, purpose and context play a key role in shaping instances of practice. He writes, "Swimming for speed will differ from swimming for aesthetic display, for fitness, for work, for relaxation, or for religious purposes" (43). His theorizations acknowledge the significance of material conditions for performers. But, a further delineation is needed for enactments that take place during performance occasions. In performance occasions, there are two layers of context. The first layer is the historical situation of the performance: swimming in Canada in the twenty-first century. The second layer is the performance activity: a swimming competition. This second layer is important because the configuration of the swimming competition shapes the purpose of the enactment for the swimmer, which likely includes swimming for speed and/or swimming to compete. Importantly, however, purpose is not the only factor that influences a swimmer's movements during a competition. Imagine that I am a swimmer. I can swim for speed in a range of situations—alone in an ocean, with friends at the pool, during a swim competition. In all of these contexts, the historical situation, areas of technique, and purpose might affect my swimming, but in a swim competition there are additional factors that influence my behaviours:

the rules. During a swimming competition, I cannot start when I choose; I must start when the starter's gun is fired. I cannot swim where I like; I must stay in my lane, and depending on the stroke, I might need to place my hands in a specific position to turn around. Akin parameters apply to performance in other genres. I can choose to recite sections of Shakespeare's *Hamlet* in a range of contexts from my living room to a university classroom to a professional stage production. In all of these contexts, my enactments might be guided by a combination of acting technique and the historical situation. But, in a conventional professional production of the play, my enactments would also be guided by the specifics of the rules, conventions, laws, and traditions of the located configuration, shaping my performance in relation to elements such as the parameters of the playing space and the blocking.

In the context of performance activities, then, practice is not only structured by technique, historical situation, or purpose; it is also structured by the conventions, rules, traditions, and laws that stitch together the behaviours and sequences of action during the performance, by activity configurations. To refer to this simultaneous structuring of an instance of practice by an area of technique and configuration, I introduce the term "formation." Unlike practice, which names a concrete instance of embodied movement, "formation" refers to the structuring principles that underpin that instance of practice. In a performance, technique *and* the rules, laws, traditions, and conventions of performance activities are to the structuring of practice as two polynucleotide strands are to the double helix of DNA. Like the two strands, an activity and an area of technique are distinct, but, in performances, they bond together to structure practice. In the same way that the intersections of the strands fuse to form a recognizable gene, in performance, technique and activity fuse to form a recognizable practice. This structuring takes place within bodies, and is, thus, deeply personal for the performer, as she must negotiate not only the area of technique and the activity configuration but also her own body's capacities, abilities, and, indeed, the edges of her body's capacities and abilities. It is also inflected by a range of factors embedded in the configuration, including level (grassroots, recreational, elite, professional, etc.), economics, and whether or not the activity is part of a performance event. As such, a formation is variable and emergent, taking place from moment to moment. This is where it becomes important that we conceptualize activity configurations as enacted by bodies (rather than as parameters that "frame" bodies). While it may seem that the rules of swimming are outside the swimmer—the lane ropes, for example, physically enclose the athlete—the act of not hitting the lane ropes and staying within the space demarcated by them is, indeed, *an act,* a bodily movement. Again, while this is important for examining sports, it is also significant for other performance activities. The practice of acting in repertory theatre in Canada and the United States, for example, is structured by acting technique and by the activity configuration of theatre. As well as acting, performers must be able to enter and exit the playing area on cue (sometimes with the help of a stage manager or assistant stage manager), execute blocking directions motivated by technical needs, and hit their marks.

In instances of practice that take place in performances, this negotiation always takes place between technique and a located configuration; in training, however, this negotiation may take place between an area of technique and a general activity configuration. Take, for example, the formation of competitive women's basketball in Canada in the early twenty-first century. The early history of basketball in Canada diverged from the development of the sport in the United States.[10] This was, in large part, due to the lack of national standardization of physical education for women in early twentieth century Canada, which resulted in rule differences across the country's different provinces.[11] By the early 1970s, however, Canadian women's basketball rules were standardized, and the rules of Canadian and American women's basketball closely resembled one another. Today, Canada Basketball—a national, not-for-profit, sport organization—oversees women's basketball in the country. Recently, Canada Basketball has adopted a framework known as "Sport for Life" in Canada, which provides a model for the transmission of practice and skills in sports. One of Sport for Life's major initiatives is to introduce the Long-Term Athlete Development (LTAD) program, a seven-stage training outline that has been adopted by most of Canada's sport-specific not-for-profit organizations. Two progressive stages of LTAD are significant for their combination of technique and activity configuration *(Canada Basketball)*. In the Learn to Train phase of basketball development, athletes learn sport-specific skills (shooting, dribbling, passing); in Train to Train, the phase that follows Learn to Train, athletes learn team-based and advanced skills (setting a screen, team offence, team defence). In Learn to Train training sessions, coaches emphasize technique; drills and modified games are used to support acquisition of technique and to downplay the significance of competition. The shift to Train to Train, for both athletes and coaches, is an increased emphasis on activity configuration. To put it plainly, when I teach a ten-year-old how to shoot a basketball, I do not worry about the activity configuration. If they shuffle their feet before shooting—an act against the rules of basketball—it is okay. The emphasis of learning is on the passage of technique from one body to another. When I coach that same player years later, however, this emphasis shifts. I prepare the player to participate in games by reminding them not to move their feet before shooting so that they will not break the rules of basketball. This shift is crucial for the athlete who wishes to participate in a game: if the player cannot structure her practice in relation to both basketball technique and activity, she will not be able to participate in basketball games where the rules are strictly enforced. Indeed, one of the purposes of training is to sediment a formation into one's body so that the act of negotiating between two structuring principles becomes instinctive. To examine the physiological, psychological, and philosophical effects of such sedimentation, I turn to the case of the formation of women's basketball in the late twentieth and early twenty-first century.

The Formation of Women's Basketball in the Early Twenty-First Century

Since the late 1960s, men's and women's basketball have been governed by a similar set of rules in the United States. Critically, during this period, the concept of a player's "cylinder" emerged as one of the major guiding principles for conceptualizing player-to-player contact in both men's and women's basketball. According to the International Basketball Federation (FIBA), the vertical cylinder is "the space within an imaginary cylinder occupied by a player on the floor. It includes the space above the player and is limited to: the front by the palms of the hands, the rear by the buttocks, and the sides by the outer edge of the arms and legs." Using the skill of throwing and the phrase "throws like a girl" as an entry point to think about bodily comportment, Iris Young describes the ways in which girls in western societies are trained in the modalities of "feminine bodily existence" (35), which includes conventions about comportment, motility, and spatiality. She writes:

> We decide beforehand - usually mistakenly – that the task is beyond us and thus give it less than our full effort. At such a half-hearted level, of course, we cannot perform the task, become frustrated, and fulfill our own prophecy. In entering a task, we frequently are self-conscious about appearing awkward and at the same time do not wish to appear too strong. Both worries contribute to our awkwardness and frustration.
> (34–35)

Young contends that if a girl does not release herself from this thought pattern, she may learn to "hamper her movements," becoming "more timid with age" (43); this will, in turn, affect how she comports herself in sports. What Young identifies is a curious cycle that combines physical repetition with its psychological and philosophical effects. For Young, what a body does, impacts what a body has done, which impacts what a body can do, which impacts what a body will do. More simply put, by not participating in sport, a girl does not develop the skills of sport, which makes her anxious about playing sports, which makes her less likely to engage in sporting activities.

Analyzing this cycle in relation to the formation of women's basketball in the twentieth century illuminates the political work that gets carried out through women's basketball practice. The specifics of physical contact in basketball are one of the activity's defining features. Unlike sports such as football, hockey, lacrosse, and rugby, where players in possession of the ball lose the right to personal space and are, therefore, susceptible to being body-checked, shoved, or tackled, the articulation of the rules of basketball emphasize the significance of an individual's right to personal space. To be successful in game situations, basketball players need to sediment several knowledges into their bodies. The basketball-specific skill of squaring up provides an indicative example. In basketball, the term "square up" is used to indicate that an offensive player holding the basketball should turn their body so that their hips and shoulders are facing the hoop. Usually, a player squares-up after receiving a pass from a teammate. The skill assumes that the offensive player will be closely defended. The defensive player's goal in this situation is to restrict the offensive player's ability to square up by crowding her space and/or trying to bat or snatch the ball out of the offensive player's hands. The situation of squaring-up—where an offensive player receives the ball and tries to face the hoop and a defensive player attempts to stop her—takes place hundreds of times in a single basketball game.

To square-up successfully, a player needs to develop strength and balance so that she can protect her space and withstand a degree of physical contact. She must also learn the technique of squaring-up, which involves pivoting with one foot planted on the ground while moving the ball from the catching position to the triple-threat position (where the ball is held at the ribs, allowing a player to shoot, pass, or dribble). Importantly, if a defensive player crowds an offensive player when she catches the ball, the offensive player must not lean away from the contact; rather, she must "rip," or move, the ball from the shooting position to the triple-threat position. She must, in short, claim her cylinder, her physical space on the court. Sometimes, this might result in contact with the defensive player, and, so, the offensive player also needs to learn to be comfortable with activity-appropriate physical contact. Significantly, a player's mental and emotional conceptualization of her right to space is integral to her ability to execute a square-up in a game. To this point, if I catch the basketball and the defensive player crowds my space, but I do not know or do not believe that I have a right to that space, I am unlikely to move, never mind risk making assertive physical contact with another human being, contact which, outside the context of the activity, might be considered inappropriate. However, if I believe I have a right to my space and am compelled by the purpose of the activity (to score baskets!), I am far more likely to risk an encounter with another body and execute the square-up.

Critically, squaring-up is one of several skills in basketball that is structured by the principle of the cylinder; other skills include posting-up, boxing-out, taking a charge, bumping a cutter, and setting a screen. These skills are performed repeatedly during a basketball game and are points of emphasis in basketball training sessions, and through the repeated structuring of practice by the formation of basketball, the principle of the cylinder may sediment into a player's body. Indeed, as someone who has played basketball for over 25 years,

I naturally square-up to the hoop when I receive the basketball on offense; it is as instinctive as walking. This is where the curious cycle Young identifies becomes important. Because claiming space is in my body physiologically (my muscles are trained for balance), psychologically (I believe I have the capacity to claim space), and philosophically (I believe I have a right to space), the principle of the cylinder may structure my movements in the world. In short, just as female bodily comportment impacts the way a woman may move in basketball, so might basketball impact the way a woman, man, or person of another gender identification, moves in the world.

To be clear, I am not suggesting that learning to protect one's space through basketball is in and of itself emancipatory for people who play women's basketball. The formation of basketball does not necessarily sediment into an individual's body; a person's participation in a performance activity is one of many (many) patterns of bodily movement that she or they performs each day, and all of these movement patterns dynamically co-mingle in her, and through her body. Moreover, what it means for a woman, man, or a person of another gender identification to claim physical space outside the context of a basketball game varies in relation to socio-cultural-historical context and an individual's matrix of identities. Nonetheless, the capacity to hold and claim space can still be a meaningful action in the early twenty-first century, and while there have undoubtedly been shifts since Young's theorizations in the late 1980s, Young's assertion that women—as well as persons who identify with femininity, agender or non-binary persons, and trans persons—are often "physically inhibited, confined, positioned and objectified" (42) still articulates traditional notions of gendered corporeality in the early twenty-first century. Moreover, despite its significance in contemporary basketball, I have yet to encounter a history of the game that acknowledges the influence of Berenson or the modified rules on the development of the principle of the vertical plane in the general configuration of contemporary basketball. This oversight is consistent with a trend in basketball history that tends to under-emphasize women's participation in the general configuration of basketball. While the modified rules were developed to contain women's bodies, Berenson's articulation appeared decades before such terminology was used elsewhere, and, as evidenced by the case of women's basketball, the vertical plane is an integral component of contemporary basketball practice. The genealogy of the vertical plane marks a clear instance of reciprocal influence between women's and men's basketball, and the concept of the vertical plane offers an indicative example of how the meanings of enactments embedded in the structuring of activities and the patterning of behaviour during these activities are as dynamic as the performances themselves. This evinces how the concepts of configuration and formation can both facilitate an analysis of the effects of embodied practice for performers and illuminate facets of performance that might otherwise remain obscured.

Notes

1 The concept of "framing" is frequently attributed to Erving Goffman; however, Goffman explicitly cites Gregory Bateson for the theoretical foundation of his work. In "A Theory of Play and Fantasy," published in 1972 as part of *Steps to an Ecology of Mind*, Bateson introduces "the psychological frame" by using two analogies: the picture frame; and a mathematical set. For Bateson, these two analogies are generative because they help negotiate the relationship between the concrete and the abstract and the relation between structure and agency. Significantly, Bateson suggests that psychological frames are metacommunicative, meaning "Any message, which either explicitly or implicitly defines a frame, ipso facto gives the received instructions or aids in his attempt to understand the messages included within the frame" (188). The metacommunicative aspect of Bateson's theory is the element that has been most broadly applied by scholars. See: Bateson.
2 Diana Taylor argues that frames are the "formulaic structures that predispose certain outcomes and yet allow for reversal, parody, and change," and suggests they are "basically fixed and, as such, repeatable and transferable" (31). Richard Schechner uses the term frame to refer to the rules or conventions that say what must or must not be done in each activity (*Performance Theory* 15). John MacAloon follows Bateson and Goffman's model of frames and applies it to his analysis of spectacle and the ramified performance type of the Olympic Games. See: Schechner *Performance Theory;* MacAloon "Rite drama festival spectacle;" Taylor.
3 For more on "scriptive things," see: Bernstein. For more on "habitus," see: Bourdieu, 169–208.
4 At the turn of the twentieth century, "women's basketball" referred to basketball that was modified for enactment by female bodies and was contrasted with "basketball," which was played by males. As I demonstrate in my discussion of modified women's basketball, this distinction influenced the genealogy of one branch of basketball in Canada and the United States. In the twenty-first century, organized basketball activities are often still divided by gender and might include boys' basketball, girls' basketball, co-ed basketball, women's basketball, and men's basketball. Participants in boys', girls', men's, co-ed, or women's basketball may identify with a range of gender identifications, including boy, girl, man, woman, non-binary, gender-fluid, or transgender. In my usage of "women's basketball," I do not mean to imply that all the players identify as women; rather, I use "women's basketball" to refer to a category of activity that is meaningfully linked to a specific branch of basketball practice.
5 The early history of women's basketball in the United States is detailed in the collection *A Century of Women's Basketball: From Frailty to Final Four*. See: Albertson; Baer and Davenport; Hult "The Governance;" Hult "The Sage; Emery and Toohey-Costa; Spears.
6 These questions have been extrapolated from the following sources: Porter 11–115; Pitts and Semenick; Podmenik, Keskosek and Erculj.
7 See: Schechner *Between Theatre and Anthropology*, pp. 1–50.
8 See: Taylor, pp. 18–122.
9 See: Roach, pp. 2–30.
10 For more on this history, see: Hall *The Girl and the Game;* Hall *The Grads Are Playing;* Vertinsky.
11 See: Hall *The Girl and the Game;* Hall *The Grads Are Playing;* Vertinsky.

References

Albertson, Roxanne M. "Basketball Texas Style, 1910–1933: School to Industrial Competition." *A Century of Women's Basketball: From Frailty to Final Four*, edited by Joan S. Hult and Marianna Trekell, 1991, pp. 155–67.

Ahmed, Sara. *Queer Phenomenology: Orientations, Objects, Others*. Duke University Press, 2006.

"Clara Gregory Baer: Catalyst for Women's Basketball." *A Century of Women's Basketball: From Frailty to Final Four*, edited by Joan S. Hult and Marianna Trekell, 1999, pp. 19–37.

Bateson, Gregory. *Steps to an Ecology of Mind*. Ballantine Bks, 1981.

Bernstein, Robin. "Toward the Integration of Theatre History and Affect Studies: Shame and the Rude Mechs's 'The Method Gun.'" *Theatre Journal*, vol. 64, no. 2, 2012, pp. 213–30.

Berenson, Senda. "The Significance of Basket Ball for Women." *Spalding Official Basket Ball Guide for Women*, edited by Senda Berensen, American Sports Publishing Co, 1905, pp. 31–45.

———, editor. *Spalding Official Basket Ball Guide for Women*. American Sports Publishing Co, 1905.

Bourdieu, Pierre. *Distinction: A Social Critique of the Judgement of Taste*. Harvard University Press, 1984.

Canada Basketball Athlete Development Model. Basketball Canada, Dec., 2008, *Canada Basketball Athlete Development Model*. Basketball Canada, December, 2008.

Davenport, Joanna. "The Tides of Change in Women's Basketball Rules." *A Century of Women's Basketball: From Frailty to Final Four*, edited by Joan S. Hult and Marianna Trekell, National Association for Girls and Women in Sport, 1991, pp. 83–108.

Dosch, Nancy Cole. "'The Sacrifice of Maidens' or Healthy Sportswomen? The Medical Debate Over Women's Basketball." *A Century of Women's Basketball: From Frailty to Final Four*, edited by Joan S. Hult and Marianna Trekell, 1991, pp. 125–37.

Emery, Lunne Fauley and Margaret Toohey-Costa. "Hoop and Skirts: Women's Basketball on the West Coast 1892–1930s." *A Century of Women's Basketball: From Frailty to Final Four*, edited by Joan S. Hult and Marianna Trekell, 1991, p. 137.

Gaine, Chris. "Remembering One of the NBA's Biggest Failed Experiments: The 'New Ball' | Complex." *Complex*, April 12, 2017, http://www.complex.com/sports/2017/04/new-ball-nba-spalding.

Goffman, Erving. *Frame Analysis: An Essay on the Organization of Experience*. 1st Northeastern University Press ed, Northeastern University Press, 1986.

Hall, Ann. *The Girl and the Game: A History of Women's Sport in Canada*. Second edition, University of Toronto Press, 2016.

———. *The Grads Are Playing Tonight! The Story of the Edmonton Commercial Graduates Basketball Club*. University of Alberta Press, 2011, http://deslibris.ca.ezproxy.library.ubc.ca/ID/452310.

Hult, Joan S. "The Governance of Athletics for Girls and Women: Leadership by Women Physical Educator." *A Century of Women's Basketball: From Frailty to Final Four*. National Association for Girls and Women in Sport, 1991, pp. 53–82.

"The Saga of Competition: Basketball Battles and Governance War," *A Century of Women's Basketball: From Frailty to Final Four*. National Association for Girls and Women in Sport, 1991, pp. 223–48.

Hult, Joan S. and Marianna Trekell, editors. *A Century of Women's Basketball: From Frailty to Final Four*. National Association for Girls and Women in Sport, 1991.

"'Configuration, n.'." *OED Online*, Oxford University Press, http://www.oed.com/view/Entry/38824?redirectedFrom=configuration.

International Basketball Federation (FIBA), "Official Basketball Rules 2020."FIBA.com, March, 2021, https://www.fiba.basketball/documents/official-basketball-rules/2020.pdf.

Basketball Canada, "LTAD." *Basketball.ca*, https://www.basketball.ca/en/development/ltad.

MacAloon, John J., et al., editors. *Rite, Drama, Festival, Spectacle: Rehearsals toward a Theory of Cultural Performance*. Institute for the Study of Human Issues, 1984.

Massumi, Brian. *Parables for the Virtual: Movement, Affect, Sensation*. Duke University Press, 2002.

Podmenik, Nadja, et al. "The Effect of Introducing a Smaller and Lighter Basketball on Female Basketball Players' Shot Accuracy." *Journal of Human Kinetics*, vol. 31, no. 1, 2012, pp. 131–7, doi:10.2478/v10078-012-0014-8.

Porter, Karra. *Mad Seasons: The Story of the First Women's Professional Basketball League, 1978–1981*. University of Nebraska Press, Lincoln, 2006.

Roach, Joseph R. *Cities of the Dead: Circum-Atlantic Performance*. Columbia University Press, 1996.

"Naismith's Rules," Naismith Basketball Foundation, https://naismithbasketballfoundation.com/about-basketball/naismiths-rules-for-basketball/.

Schechner, Richard. *Between Theater & Anthropology*. University of Pennsylvania Press, 1985.

Spatz, Ben. *What a Body Can Do: Technique as Knowledge, Practice as Research*. Routledge, Taylor & Francis Group, 2015.

Spears, Betty. "Sena Berenson Abbott: New Woman, New Sport," *A Century of Women's Basketball: From Frailty to Final Four*. National Association for Girls and Women in Sport, 1991, pp. 19–36.

Stanaland, Peggy, "The Early Years of Basketball in Kentucky," *A Century of Women's Basketball: From Frailty to Final Four*, edited by Joan S. Hult and Marianna Trekell, 1991.

Steveda, Chepko. "The Sacrifice of Maidens or Healthy Sportswomen? The Medical Debate Over Women's Basketball," *A Century of Women's Basketball: From Frailty to Final Four*, edited by Joan S. Hult and Marianna Trekell, 1991, pp. 109–24.

Turner, Victor W. *The Ritual Process: Structure and Anti-Structure*. Aldine Pub. Co, 1969.

Vertinsky, Patricia. *Disciplining Bodies in the Gymnasium: Memory, Monument, Modernism*. Routledge, 2004.

Young, Iris Marion. *On Female Body Experience: "Throwing Like a Girl" and Other Essays*. Oxford University Press, 2005.

3
THE PATTERNING OF AUDIENCE BEHAVIOURS AND HOCKEY IN CANADA

It is the final day of the 2010 Winter Olympic Games in Vancouver. Closed to normal traffic, the downtown streets are filled with people.[1] They stand shoulder to shoulder, facing gigantic outdoor screens. On the screens, the men's gold medal hockey game, featuring Canada and the United States is projected. Seven minutes into the overtime period, the puck is in the American offensive zone. Canadian player Sidney Crosby takes a shot. It bounces off American goalie Zach Parise's pad and toward the corner. Crosby's teammate Jarome Iginla retrieves the puck. He's closely guarded. Crosby skates toward the goal. Iginla fends off his defender and passes the puck to Crosby. At precisely the right moment, Crosby shifts his weight, moving his stick from behind him to in front of him, and directs the puck toward the goal. It sails past Parise and hits the back of the net. In the stadium and on the street. Canadian audience members erupt, cheering, screaming, high-fiving, and hugging one another. Why did they perform this set of behaviours? What gets carried out through gestures such as clapping and yelling? How did the practice of high-fiving contribute to a performance of intersubjectivity? Whereas the last chapter focussed on sporting activities and the structuring of specialized areas of embodied practice for individual performers (athletes), this chapter responds to the above questions by examining sporting events and the structuring of practice for audience members. To do so, I apply the concepts of configuration and formation to the study of audience behaviours.

Typically, performance events are conceptualized as unified happenings that involve an encounter between two groups of people: one group who enacts specialized skills as part of an occasion that is demarcated from everyday life (performers) and a second group who participates in the occasion by acknowledging these enactments (audience members).[2] This conceptualization works

DOI: 10.4324/9781003275879-4

for performance genres where one of the purposes for performers is display or where the activity implies an audience such as western conservatory theatre productions, classical music concerts, stand-up comedy shows, and burlesque performances. In performance genres where the formal features of the genre are such that an audience is not implied by the activity configuration—soccer games, sailing races, and chess games—it is useful to unsettle a notion of a unified happening. I, therefore, propose an approach that builds traditional conceptualizations and emphasizes the relations between these groupings in terms of the patterning of behaviour. Instead of conceptualizing performance events as unified happenings where the behaviours and actions of multiple groups of people are stitched together by a single-set of conventions, traditions, laws, and rules, I view performance events as occasions where two or more groups of individuals come together to enact distinct but interconnected configurations.

In this framework, all participants are performers in the broad sense of the term; actors, dancers, audience members, stage managers, athletes, light operators, musicians, security guards, circus performers, masters of ceremonies, judges, coaches, and music conductors all perform behaviours. But there are important distinctions between in the patterning of behaviour of different participants. For example, in contemporary circus events, circus performers, audience members, and ushers are all perform, but the specific behaviours are patterned by distinct located configurations: circus performers enact specialized areas of practice that emphasize the display of skills; audience members witness and respond to the enactment of distinct areas of practice; and ushers mediate and support by directing spectators to their seats and overseeing audience behaviours. Similarly, a recreational hockey event might include players, officials, and audience members wherein the players perform specialized skills with the aim of competing against others, officials oversee the enactment of skills and competition, and audience members observe and react to the performances of the players and officials.

Importantly, even though the behaviours of hockey audience members are influenced by the sporting action, the general hockey configuration does not pattern the behaviours of audience members. Hockey games can, and are, played without spectators. Of course, there are instances— and indeed entire genres of performance—where the boundaries between performance event groups are blurred; twenty-first century participatory and immersive performances often intentionally unsettle the distinctions between event participant groups, and they often do so by inviting cross-pollination between elements of performance configurations, such as the conventions that typically demarcate the audience space from the playing space. Moreover, an individual or group of individuals may move between performance groupings during an occasion: in a recreational hockey game, an audience member might become a performer if another player is needed; in a theatre show, an usher may become an audience member when they have completed their duties.

There is a rich body of theatre studies work that examines audience members as active performance event participants,[3] and the behaviours of audience members in performance genres such as site-specific and socially engaged theatre, in particular, have increasingly been theorized through the lens of performance and participation.[4] Critically, however, such works have predominantly examined performing arts audiences and have infrequently examined the details of the patterning of audience behaviours. While "traditional" audience behaviours such as clapping may appear relatively static when compared to the dynamic movements that may be prompted by participatory performance genres, actions such as clapping and cheering are "concrete examples of actions, moments of doing, historical instances of materialized activity" (Spatz 41); they are, in other words, practice. My theorizations focus on sport, but this is the case across performance genres, from socially engaged performance to contemporary dance. To explore the relationship between audience performance and sporting activities, I examine hockey audiences in Canada. As David Whitson and Richard Gruneau suggest, hockey has become one of Canada's "most significant collective representations—a story that Canadians tell themselves about what it means to be Canadian" (13). In investigating the patterning of audience behaviours over time I illustrate how shifting audience practices contribute to, and transform, hockey's position in Canada's national imaginary.

The Emergence of Hockey Audience Practices

While a broad conceptualization of audience, such as the one found in *The Oxford English Dictionary,* might define an audience as "[a]ll the people within hearing of something; (hence) the assembled listeners or spectators at a public performance or event (as a play, film, lecture, etc.) considered collectively" ("audience, n"), these parameters are too general for the purposes of examining the patterning of behaviour in sporting events. I can stand at the top of a community hockey rink chatting with a friend and mentally recognize that a hockey game is taking place on the ice below, but it is not until I physically turn toward the playing space and acknowledge the sporting action that I enact an element of the audience configuration and participate in the constitution of the performance event. As such, for the purposes of studying the patterning of behaviours in sporting events, "audience" is defined as all the individuals who recognize a sport performance activity by consciously enacting a set of behaviours stitched together by a configuration. Audience configurations emerge in relation to concrete occasions and coalesce into recognizable sets of behaviours and actions over time. Because of this, spectating practices vary by sport, location, and time period. For instance, golf spectators in Canada and the United States conventionally remain silent during sporting action and applaud following exceptional skill execution; whereas association football spectators in Europe typically make noise during the action and cheer enthusiastically when goals are scored. Despite such distinctions, sporting audience configurations share two key features.

First, sporting audience configurations emerge in relation to one another. The development of the hockey audience configuration in the late nineteenth century offers an indicative example. A range of physical contests and sporting activities existed in Canada at this time; these included swimming, running, boxing, baseball, lacrosse[5] and several stick and ball games on ice, such as shinny, an on-ice adaptation of the Scottish game shinty, and tooadijik, a Mi'kmaq game (Venuum; Rand 181). People regularly watched these contests, so when the first recognized indoor ice hockey game took place in March 1875, the conventions, rules, traditions, and laws that stitched together these spectating practices along with those in other physical contests shaped the audience behaviours of indoor ice hockey. Individuals oriented themselves toward the playing space and recognized the game by following the sporting action.

Second, specific elements of an audience configuration are anchored to the specific features of sporting activity configurations. As is evident from the demarcation of space, the orientation of spectators, and the segmentation of time, the general principles of hockey functioned as anchors for the conventions, rules, traditions, and laws of the hockey audience configuration. A report of the first recognized indoor ice hockey game (hereafter, simply, hockey), in *The Montreal Gazette*, described this match as a "novel contest on ice" that was "like lacrosse in one sense—the block having to move through flags placed about 8 feet apart in the same manner as the rubble ball—but in the main the old country game of shinty gives the best idea of hockey" (qtd. in Gruneau and Whitson, 38). By 1886, the "novel contest" of hockey was popular enough that a championship tournament was organized, and in 1887, *The Montreal Gazette* published the "Playing Rules for the Game of Hockey" (Zeisler xix). While the rules of hockey in the late nineteenth and early twentieth century differed markedly from the twenty-first-century rules, the general principles of hockey have remained stable since the publication of these rules: two teams of players use sticks to direct an object—originally a ball, then a block, later a puck—across an oval-shaped ice-covered playing surface and into the opponent's goal. The object of the game is to score as many goals as possible; with the exception of brief pauses for rule infractions or after the scoring of goals, action is continuous, and players are permitted to engage in physical contact but barred from tackling, charging from behind, tripping, or kicking other participants.

From its inception, the ice-covered playing space of hockey was designated for athletes and officials only. As such, audience members were positioned

FIGURE 3.1 Hockey Match, Victoria Rink, Montreal, QC, composite, 1893, painted by George Horne Russell and photographed by Wm. Notman & Son.

outside of the activity. Because of the shape of the playing space (an oval with nets at either end), the purpose of the activity (to score goals), and the orientation of players during a game (in relation to the puck, the nets, and each other), hockey audience configurations tended to surround the playing space, and, by consequence, spectators could see the game and each other. Moreover, hockey was (and is) a dynamic game where players continuously move across a relatively large playing space. Alongside a spectator's general orientation (toward the playing space, beside other spectators), the dynamic, continuous action of hockey prompted (and prompts) uninterrupted micro-orientations, as audience members choose where to focus their attention. Audience members have several micro-orientation options: they can choose to watch the section of the ice closest to them, follow the movement of the puck, follow the movement of a specific player, follow a cluster of players, or choose to turn their bodies and their attention away from the game. While an individual might have chosen any of these orientations, photographs and paintings suggest that, by the early twentieth century, hockey spectators conventionally focussed their attention on the movement of the puck and the players closest to it.

Finally, the temporal demarcations and rhythms of a hockey game influenced the temporal demarcations and rhythms of the hockey audience configuration. While the third period was not added until 1910, hockey has always sequenced action into extended segments (30 segments before 1910; 20 minutes after 1910). The hockey audience configuration followed this temporal segmentation. Within these broad sequences of action, the play of hockey involved continuous action with occasional stoppages in play (for penalties or goals); consequently, the conventional rhythm of hockey audience spectating involved alternation between active, engaged, physical recognition, (micro-orientations) and rest.

As with sporting activities, performance audience practices are simultaneously patterned by audience configurations and by areas of technique. Conventional audience practices such as sitting, standing, clapping, high-fiving, hugging, fist-pumping, cheering, yelling, booing, and jeering are structured by areas of technique that can be categorized as "non-specialized" and "everyday." They also belong to the broad category of sporting audience practices. Sporting audience practices are necessarily relational; audience members sit, clap, cheer, and jeer in relation to the enactments of a sport performance. Following this, the purpose that underpins the areas of technique that structure sporting audience practices is to manifest the relationship between audience member and performer. As a hockey audience member, I clap to demonstrate my acknowledgement of an exceptional moment of physical execution, jeer to manifest my negative emotional response to a moment in the action, or cheer to evince my support of a player or a team, etc. Importantly, because of the chain that connects audience practices to activity configurations, the customary behaviours that manifest the relationship between audience member and performer vary by cultural context and sport. As noted above, in a twenty-first professional golf tournament in the United States audience members acknowledge the action by remaining silent during a shot.

In concrete instances, areas of technique and hockey audience configurations combine to structure hockey audience practices; this is an audience formation. Importantly, audience formations structure practice through two inter-connected processes. The first of these processes emerges from the co-mingling of the purpose underpinning areas of sporting audience technique and the encounters prompted by hockey audience configurations. One of the effects of an audience configuration is that it produces a dynamic matrix of encounters between spectators, performers, and objects: spectators encounter the players, the playing space, the puck, the sticks, the action, the officials, and other spectators. In hockey, these encounters have both physiological and mental effects. On the one hand, hockey is a dynamic game that involves colour, movement, sound, and physical sensations (the temperature of the air, the pressure of a seat against one's body, etc.). Even with a limited understanding of the game itself, a spectator's encounter with this meshwork of stimuli is likely to prompt physiological responses that shape the visceral dimension of their experience. On the other hand, even when hockey was first emerging as a distinct and recognizable sport in the late nineteenth and early twentieth centuries, most (if not all) audience members would have recognized hockey as a performance (an activity demarcated from everyday life) and as a physical contest involving the display of specialized skills (as a sport). The intellectual recognition of hockey as a sport lays the groundwork for the spectators' encounters with each other as a grouping of performance participants gathered to acknowledge an activity, and for what Lev Kreft calls "the drama of sport." Kreft explains:

> The source of the dramatic in sport is that sport games are among disjunctive games which demand active personal (individual or collective) involvement, risk, and body movement towards a goal which is reached at a stage when all actors get their comparative value measured. To accept such risk freely, without any real pressure to do so, as in other parts of everyday life where we cannot decide even if we want to be involved, is nobility of decision to start: one starts because it is attractive, not because one has to. What follows is a real life drama, more or less complex, but always personally disjunctive, existentially challenging and aesthetically attractive.
>
> (232)

In the case of hockey, the rules and purpose of the game help to shape the specific manifestation of this drama. Players undertake personal involvement, risk, and bodily movement in pursuit of the objective of the game (to score goals) which, when reached, measures the players' value within the context of the activity.

The drama of hockey potentially prompts four related, but distinct, kinds of encounters for early twentieth-century spectators. First, during a hockey game, spectators encounter multiple instances of superb specialized skill enactments such as a pass, a goalie's save, or a shot. Even for an audience member who is not personally invested in a game's outcome, a human body successfully enacting specialized skills, such as a slapshot, might impress itself on the spectator. Second, the rhythm of the drama of hockey is predicated on a series of dynamic and continuous successes and failures: a player successfully passes the puck to his or her teammate; the teammate skates with the puck; an opponent attempts, but fails, to stop the teammate; the teammate shoots; the goalie makes a save (success for the goalie; failure for the opposing teammate); etc. As such, during a hockey game, audience members encounter a series of micro-victories and micro-defeats. Third, audience members who understand the drama of hockey can recognize critical moments within the drama. A spectator does not have to be personally invested in a player or team to appreciate the meaning of goal scoring. Fourth, because of the rules regarding physical contact and aggression, spectators encounter an activity that involves body to body contact between players and sometimes involves violence. This leads to the final encounter between hockey audience members and the sporting action. As hockey scholars such as Michael Robidoux, Richard Gruneau, and David Whitson have compellingly analyzed, hockey's ice-covered playing surface, its dynamic action, and its rules pertaining to physical contact and roughness "enabled Canadians to display qualities that have been valued in patriarchal relations: stoicism, courage, perseverance, and proficiency" (Robidoux, "Imagining" 222). In addition to the concrete aspects of the sporting action, then, hockey audience members also encounter the ideologies displayed through the enactment of hockey's configuration.

During a turn of the twentieth-century hockey game, the matrix of encounters provoked by the hockey audience configuration co-mingled with the purpose that underpinned the areas of technique that structured spectating practices (to make the relation between audience and performer manifest through action), and this co-mingling patterned the enactment of audience practice. For example, one way to manifest a relation to goal scoring, a moment of meaningful sporting action, is to applaud or cheer. To be clear, audience members did not have to applaud or cheer. Individuals bring unique knowledges, memories, experiences, and investments to their audience enactments, and there are a range of behaviours an individual might perform. Nonetheless, one conventional way of acknowledging goal scoring is to clap and make noise. Crucially, in behaving in relation to the sporting action, audience members also manifested a relation toward the ideologies that underpinned the enactment of hockey games. This does not mean that all audience members behaved in the same manner or manifested the same relation to the sporting action or such ideologies. As Robidoux argues, the male, white, able-bodied, "physically dominant, heterosexist, and capitalist associations" of hockey are exclusionary (Robidoux 222) and there were undoubtedly audience members who manifested their relation to a game by refusing to cheer, by turning away from the action, or by otherwise subverting conventional hockey audience practices.

Affect theory provides a useful set of key terms and ideas for analyzing the second way that audience formations structure audience practices in the late nineteenth and early twentieth centuries. Following what Patricia Clough calls "the affective turn" in the academy in the late 1990s and early 2000s, there are many theories of affect, and in their introduction to *The Affect Theory Reader*, Melissa Gregg and Gregory J. Seigworth identify eight "orientations that undulate and sometimes overlap in their approaches to affect" (6). These include:

> The study of human/non-human nature in the Humanities and social sciences; the boundaries of human/non-human (such as cybernetics); philosophically inflected cultural studies; philosophically inflected psychological and psychoanalytic inquiry; cultural materialism in politically engaged work, which uses affect to turn away from the linguistic turn, discourses of emotions, and finally practices in the sciences which 'embrace a pluralist approach to materialism'.
>
> (8)

One of the central threads that links these orientations to affect is the concept of the encounter: for Gilles Deleuze and Félix Guattari, affect is what is produced when two bodies encounter one another (*A Thousand Plateaus* 257); for Brian Massumi, affect is what is produced when two bodies encounter one another in the realm of the virtual, meaning the realm of potential (91–4); for Sylvan Tomkins, Eve Sedgwick, and Adam Frank affect is a human, biological, response to an encounter with stimuli (as opposed to the human biographical interpretation of that response, which might be described as emotion) (1–20); and for phenomenologists like Sara Ahmed, affective investments are forged by repeated orientations toward, and encounters with, phenomena (*Cultural Politics*; *Happiness*). While affect theorists frequently attend to encounters that involve at least one human body, the encounters that produce affect could involve organisms, animals, human bodies, objects, matter, or any combination of the above.

The visceral, mental, and ideological encounters prompted by the hockey audience configuration in the late nineteenth century potentially provoked affective processes wherein a stimulus or key moment of action may have impressed itself upon a spectator, cueing a translation process from encounter to affect to feeling (or emotion or thought). In conjunction with conventional sport spectating practices, spectators may have expressed the effect of this translation process through gestures and behaviours. For example, an instance of exceptional physical execution might impress itself on an individual, triggering an affective process that results in a behaviour that manifests the relation between audience and performer in a gasp, clap, or cheer. Or, an audience member might encounter a significant instance within the drama of hockey, such as a penalty, and this significant instance might cue an affective process that prompts an emotion (frustration with the referee, for example) which might in turn be expressed through practices such as jeering, booing, or yelling. In summary, then, hockey audience formations shape hockey audience practices by: 1. prompting a matrix of encounters between audiences and the sporting action; and 2. by cueing affective processes. Importantly, as with performer formations, audience formations shape the experiences, knowledges, and investments that get carried out through the enactment of practice, and, as I examine in the next section, audience formations shaped the enactment of intersubjectivity during hockey games in the early twenty-first century.

Audience Practices in the Early Twentieth Century

In the early nineteenth century, hockey was most popular in eastern provinces, but, as Richard Gruneau and David Whitson argue, by the early twentieth century, most "Canadian communities contained at least one commercially operated ice arena where games were played throughout the winter months"

(*Hockey Night* 55). These arenas were important for two reasons. First, they functioned as gathering hubs where people from the same neighbourhood or community could meet in an enclosed physical location. In attending a hockey game, individuals had an opportunity to see, be seen by, and interact with other community members. By arriving at the same location (the hockey rink) at approximately the same time (game time), individuals made their local communities visible, tangible, and, importantly, co-constituted. This prompted a performance, where gathering to see, interacting with, and behaving alongside others temporarily brought community into being. Second, following the hockey audience formation, spectators expressed their affective responses to the action or manifested their recognition of the activity alongside one another. Of course, responses were not necessarily cohesive or unified within the rink. Indeed, the community brought into being by a relation to the hockey action was frequently divided by competition or by affiliations with specific teams and players, and hockey games could, and frequently did, prompt the creation of multiple communities within the rink. Nevertheless, even when people behaved differently—for example, if one spectator clapped while another sighed and slumped while another booed—their behaviours still manifested a mutual relation to the sporting action.

The significance of these behaviours and the likelihood audience members might enact similar behaviours was heightened by the conditions of local hockey spectatorship during this period. In the early twentieth century, audience members and performers (players, officials, coaches) frequently had personal relationships with one another. As Gruneau and Whitson suggest, cheering "for the home team in the early years of organized baseball, hockey, or lacrosse meant cheering for teams that were likely to be composed of family, friends, or at least acquaintances" (*Hockey Night* 67). A spectator who personally knows and/or cares about a player is more likely to be invested in the outcome of an activity that ranks that player's performance at its conclusion. As such, these personal relationships strengthened the affective attachment between audience members and performers. They also amplified the bonds between audience members, as it was likely that investments in players, coaches, and teams were shared amongst spectators. Following the formation of hockey, these shared affective investments increased the likelihood that audience members would enact similar gestures and behaviours in response to the sporting action: you and I have chosen to participate in a sport performance event by enacting an activity configuration; we both know and care about the players on the local team; we are both invested in the players and, by consequence, the team's success; as such, it is likely that instances of player or team success will prompt similar affective processes that may be expressed through homologous practices such as cheering or applauding. This did not mean that all spectators experienced, behaved, or expressed themselves in the same manner. Audience formations are deeply personal, and practice is always inflected by the unique abilities, experiences, knowledges, and memories of individual bodies. And, again, hockey games could prompt the creation of multiple mini-communities within the rink. It did mean, however, that the probability that some audience members might enact similar gestures was augmented. Through these enactments, spectators manifested their intersubjective relation to the game, making it visible, audible, and sometimes sensed (like when the rafters shake during raucous celebrations).

Importantly, following the encounters prompted by hockey audience formations, audience members did not only manifest an intersubjective relation to the sporting action, they also manifested an intersubjective relation toward the ideologies enacted during the sporting action. Again, the specific relations of individual audience members differed; one person might support and be excited by the patriarchal values displayed during the game while another might be bewildered by the enactment of such values. Either way, by patterning one's behaviour in accordance with spectating technique and the hockey audience configuration (the hockey audience formation), audience members were drawn into relations with one another. Importantly, they were also drawn into a relation with the link between the ideologies enacted during the game and Canadian identity. The ideologies enacted and displayed during hockey games resonated with majoritarian conceptions of Canadian identity. As Robidoux argues, "The singularity of the game and the manner in which it was played were critical for a young and disparate nation to have as its own as it faced encroaching social, political, and cultural interests from Europe and the United States" (222). By the early twentieth century, the link between hockey and nation was strengthening and the intersubjective enactments that took place at community hockey rinks were already beginning to be inflected by Canadian nationalism. This inflection was intensified by the introduction of broadcast technologies in the mid twentieth century.

Shifting Audiences in the Mid-Twentieth Century

There is a significant corpus of work that examines the history of Canadian hockey and its position in Canada's popular cultural imaginary.[6] Such studies have acknowledged how Canadian hockey games can prompt powerful experiences of community for audience members, but they have often under-theorized the role that the patterning of audience behaviour plays in shaping these experiences. To understand the significance of audience enactments, it is necessary to contextualize the development of hockey audience practices in Canada in the twentieth century. Early twentieth century audiences had to be gathered in the same location at the same time in order to take part in the sport performance. The developments of mass broadcast technologies in the early and mid-twentieth century changed this. As a result of radio and television, sporting audience members could be dispersed across geographical locations. The critical taxonomy proposed by Nicholas Abercrombie and Brian Longhurt is useful for thinking through different kinds of audiences prompted by these technologies. Analyzing the changing spectating practices of the twentieth century, Abercrombie and Longhurst offer three key terms for differentiating between audience types: simple audience, mass audience, and diffused audience. The simple audience is a group of spectators gathered in the same geographical location to watch performers; in terms of the patterning of behaviour, it is the audience that enacts an audience configuration. The mass audience refers to spectators who are scattered across different geographical locations and access the performance through technologies such as television or radio. It is comprised of innumerable simple audiences. The diffused audience is a fragmented and media-saturated audience where representations such as jumbo-screens, digital billboards, and memes continually surround individuals. Conceptualized in terms of Guy Debord's spectacle theory, in the diffused audience "everyone becomes an audience all of the time" (68). In the case of hockey games in Canada, the radio broadcast prompted the creation of a mass audience and increased the number of people orienting towards hockey games from the hundreds or thousands inside an arena to millions across diverse geographical locations. These technologies also positioned hockey games as the centre of complex audience ecologies comprised of performance event audiences inside the stadium, innumerable simple audiences, and the overall mass audiences; just as importantly, games could be transmitted to homes, cars, coffee shops, or bars, where they might be incorporated into the background of ordinary life. This functioned to blur the boundary between demarcated occasions and everyday life.

Mass audiences and the ecologies they prompted pose a challenge for performance studies scholars. Following Peggy Phelan's assertion that "Performance's only life is in the present" (146), liveness has frequently been conceptualized as an encounter between two sets of bodies—performing bodies and spectating bodies—where both sets of bodies are spatially and temporally co-present with one another. The technological transmission of such an encounter disrupts this arrangement, and, by consequence, the simple audience inside a hockey arena is distinct from the mass television audience. Philip Auslander refutes Phelan's position, arguing that because "liveness was made visible only by the possibility of technical reproduction" (*Liveness* 54), technological advancement constantly shifts the terms by which liveness is defined. Writing about broadcast television specifically, he argues, "whereas, classically, only situations involving the physical and temporal co-presence of performers and spectators could be considered live performances, broadcasts in which the audience observes what is happening in real time but is not physically present at the event are routinely called 'live,' thus expanding the concept's referents" ("Liveness" 154). Rebecca Schneider further complicates both Phelan's and Auslander's conceptualizations of liveness through the introduction of the term "inter(in)animation." Drawing from Fred Moten, Schneider uses the term "inter(in)animation" to refer to instances where "live art and media of mechanical and technological reproduction, such as photography, cross-identify, and, more radically, cross-constitute and "improvise" each other" (7). Building from Elizabeth Freeman's notion of temporal drag, Schneider examines how inter(in)animation can prompt experiences punctuated by multiple temporalities (15), a phenomenon she refers to as "syncopated time" (2). These theorizations lead Schneider to explore a genealogy of performance that puts statues, tableau vivants, photos, performance art, re-enactment (and other phenomena) in conversation with one another.

Phelan, Auslander, and Schneider helpfully parse out the historical and temporal dimensions of conceptualizations of liveness, providing important groundwork for theorizing the impacts of broadcast technologies for hockey audiences. Critically, however, while each approach can be extended for broader application, all three authors predominantly theorize the encounter between performers or between performance and audience member. Focussing on the relations between audience members, I build from these approaches by revisiting an implicit but under-theorized element of the patterning of behaviour in "classic" live situations: co-orientation. As evidenced by the hockey audience configuration, co-orientation plays an important role in patterning audience behaviours. In non-aesthetic genres such as sport or games, performers may not be oriented toward spectators, but audience members are almost always oriented toward the performer and/or the playing space (in the case of a video game, for example). In aesthetic performance genres that emphasize display, such as theatre or dance, performers and spectators are often explicitly or implicitly oriented toward each other: the actor or dancer faces the audience, the lighting cue is designed to impact the spectator, etc. Even in the case of the more complex genealogy of encounters theorized by Rebecca Schneider, which includes tableau vivants, statues, and photographs, audience members potentially become co-oriented with each other through their shared response to the hail of the performance or phenomena. While there are, undoubtedly, exceptions to this—particularly in avant-garde and performance art, where tradition is frequently intentionally unsettled—co-orientation between spectators is often a critical, if implied, element of the encounters prompted during performance events.

This has two important implications for studying mid-twentieth century hockey audiences. First, it helps explicate relations between the mass and simple audiences prompted by the broadcast technologies. In the late twentieth century, audience enactments continued to perform intersubjectivity through the structuring of audience practice, but, in professional and elite international games, these performances were increasingly complicated by the imagined relations between audiences. As argued above, the community of the simple audience is forged through physical encounters between concrete bodies who choose to gather at the same time, in the same location, to enact hockey audience practices. Mass broadcast audiences lack physical co-presence, but audience members remain connected by co-temporal co-orientation. The effect of this is significant. As television scholar David Kennedy argues, "The knowledge that one is watching the same programme at the same time as millions of others is directly connected to the cultural commonality television can provide and creates an audience, though an audience without a presence" (6). In the mass audience, the knowledge of co-temporal co-orientation can function to prompt imagined encounters between individuals. As such, while hockey's mass "audience without a presence" (Kennedy 6) may not directly encounter the visceral features of hockey's drama (the sounds, smells, and colours of an in-arena game), they may have encountered an imagined community of national spectators. Importantly, the performance audience inside the stadium is also aware of the audience ecology prompted by a hockey game, and just as spectators in the mass audience might imagine themselves as participants in a larger audience, performance audience members might also imagine themselves as members of the mass audience.

Second, the co-orientations of mass audiences expanded the intersubjective enactments of hockey audiences from a local to a national scale. Explaining her conceptualization of alignment, Sara Ahmed writes, "The lines we follow might ... function as forms of 'alignment,' or as ways of being in line with others. We might say that we are oriented when we are in line. We are 'in line' when we face the direction that is already faced by others" (15). She continues:

> We might be used to thinking of direction as simply which way we turn, or which way we are facing, at this or that moment in time ... But what if direction, as the way we face as well as move, is organized rather than casual? We might speak then of collective direction: of ways in which nations or other imagined communities might be 'going in a certain direction' or facing the same way ...
>
> (5)

Through the large-scale co-orientation that broadcast technologies facilitated, hockey games became landmarks for nation-wide alignment. The 1972 Summit Series, an eight-game competition between the Canadian and USSR men's national teams, is an illustrative example. Played in the middle of the Cold War, the series was infused by a range of factors, including international politics, the relationship between international and professional hockey, and debates regarding best hockey training practices. The final game of the series was played in the Soviet Union, but its mass broadcast prompted the creation of thousands of simple audiences in Canada. While exact numbers cannot be tracked, estimates suggest that between 13 and 18 million of Canada's

22-million-person population tuned into the game (Zelkovich). During the game, millions of Canadian were aligned with one another through their orientation toward the game and through their behaviours. This simultaneously positioned the game as an important landmark in the Canadian cultural imaginary and bolstered the proliferation of the majoritarian ideals performed during the game. While the 1972 Summit Series offers a high-profile example of the mass co-temporal, co-orientations prompted by Canadian hockey games, it is one of thousands of broadcast hockey games that took place during the mid-twentieth century. During this period, the real-time relations between simple audiences were primarily forged through imagined intersubjective enactments between audience members scattered across different geographical locations. In the early twenty-first century, this shifted.

Hockey Audience Formation in the Early Twenty-First Century

Published in French in the late 1960s and in English in the early 1970s, Guy Debord's *Society of the Spectacle* argues that spectacle is a condition of contemporary society wherein the production and circulation of images have transformed "all that once was directly lived" into "mere representation" (Debord 1970, 1). From a twenty-first century vantage point, Debord's theorizations verge on the prophetic: the circulation of images in print culture, film, and television in the 1960s and 1970s represent a fraction of the images that circulate via print culture, film, television, the Internet, digital technologies, and mobile networks in the early twenty-first century. Following Debord, who argues that spectacle erodes social relations between individuals, the spectacularization of culture is frequently approached with suspicion by cultural theorists. John MacAloon, however, challenges Debord's conceptualization of spectacle. For MacAloon, the spectacle is "neither good nor bad, neither liberating nor alienating" (101); rather, it is a distinct form of performance with four features: grandeur, an emphasis on looking, a dynamic form which involves action, and the bicameral presence of audience and actors (80–1). Following this conceptualization, MacAloon contends that "Debord's thesis is marred by his refusal to distinguish spectacle as an organized genre of performance from the ways in which social life in general is *like* a spectacle and affords an environment within which the spectacle grows" (101). For the purposes of examining the patterning of behaviour in performance events, my approach to spectacle lies at the intersection of these two theories of spectacle.

From cellphones, tablets, and laptop computers to the proliferation of television screens in public spaces like schools and train stations, to giant screens in urban centres, a constant stream of images bombards contemporary individuals. At the same time, professional and large-scale elite performances (sport and otherwise) use a range of technologies, including amplified sound, projection, pyro-technics, large screens, and fog machines, to increase the grandeur of events. Vancouver NHL games, for example, introduce the players through a combination of video, arena-wide surround sounds, strobing lights, and on-ice projections. Alongside the size of the audiences—the Vancouver Canucks averaged approximately 17, 285 spectators per game in the 2020-2021 season (ESPN—these technical and artistic elements turn regular sporting performances into sport spectacles. Importantly, however, not all sporting events are spectacles. Recreational and competitive non-elite hockey, for example, rarely use technology such as fog machines or jumbo screens. As such, specific hockey audience practices vary by level and context, depending on the co-mingling of technique with a located activity configuration. For example, whereas audience members in recreational hockey games primarily orient toward the playing space and the sporting action, audience members in a professional hockey event orient toward the playing space and the jumbo-screen where sporting, and other, action is frequently projected.

The rapid development of telecommunication technologies influenced the emergence of new spectating techniques in the early twenty-first century. Between 1987 and 2010, the number of cell phone users in Canada increased from 100, 000 to 24 million (Health Canada). By 2008, most of these phones came equipped with cameras that could connect to the Internet, take photographs, and record short videos. Such technologies prompted a new area of technique: smartphone technique. The area of smartphone technique involved a range of skills, from typing on a small keyboard to interacting with the phone's user interface to taking photographs with the phone's technologies. Unlike performance genres such as theatre, where convention, and sometimes rules or laws, discourage audience members from using phones during performances, the use of phones is not discouraged at sporting events. As such, spectators began using their cell phones to capture photos, audio, and video during the events themselves. By adding a new area of technique to the formations that underpin sport spectatorship, new audience practices such as handling one's phone to send or check messages and holding one's phone in the air to take video or photographs emerged.

In hockey, as in other sports, these practices shifted spectatorship conditions in small, but significant ways. Cell and smart phones provided a new anchor towards which audience members might orient their bodies and attention. During a game, audience members might alternate their attention and bodies between the playing space, the jumbo-screens (in professional hockey), other audience members, and their phones. This allowed, and even encouraged, individuals to oscillate their attention between the elements of the performance event and their ordinary lives. It is easy to read this oscillation through the lens of distraction: cell and smart phones draw audience member attention away from the game and in doing so disrupt their immersion in the performance event. Importantly, however, sporting audience members conventionally cross in and out of the threshold that demarcates an occasion from ordinary life. As such, a person staring at their phone is no different from a person holding an unrelated conversation throughout the game; both are physically present in the event space but neither enacts apparently typical audience practices. Cell and smart phones may have increased the quantity and visibility of such persons and this may have affected the composition of the general audience grouping, but they did not fundamentally alter the parameters that define a performance audience as a category of participants whose behaviours are stitched together by a distinct configuration. Rather, cell and smart phones shifted the effects of spectating practices enacted during hockey games by allowing audience members to record their experiences and by facilitating a more porous relationship between the demarcation of the performance event and everyday life.

While hockey differs from the phenomena at the centre of Rebecca Schneider's analyses (re-enactments, photographs, performance art), the logic of inter(in)animation and syncopated time helps unpack the effects of twenty-first century audience formations. Through the lens of inter(in)animation, which considers how a range of phenomena can prompt experiences of syncopated time, the technologies of the broadcast configuration and the gestures and behaviours of hockey audience members layered temporalities prior to the emergence of smartphone technologies. Smartphone technologies, however, added another site for the provocation of temporally syncopated experiences and potentially increased the future-oriented layer of these experiences. Taking a picture, recording audio, or filming a hockey game to a phone's memory card is a future-oriented action; I record the present so that I or someone else may view it later. Through the logic of technological reproduction, then, the future potentially punctuates a hockey spectator's experience of the present during twenty-first century hockey games. At the same time, the communication capabilities of cell and smart phones further expanded a spectator's sense of the present. When my phone buzzes, the world outside the performance event momentarily asserts itself into the world of the performance event, potentially increasing the capaciousness of my experience of the present. Critically, in the mid-2000s, this potential was heightened by the popularization of social networking sites with user-generated content such as Facebook (2004), YouTube (2005), Twitter (2006), and Tumblr (2007). Amongst many other features, these sites allowed users to share content (text, images, audio, and video) with groups of others and with the public. In combination with cell and smartphone technologies, these sites allowed people to communicate to groups of people across geographic space and to connect with a broad experience of the present. These shifts are critical because they contribute to hockey's continued place in Canada's contemporary cultural imaginary.

The men's gold medal game at the Vancouver 2010 Olympics is an illustrative example. While the International Olympic Committee (IOC) and the

Vancouver Organizing Committee (VANOC) may have attempted to shape the celebratory mood before and after the 2010 men's gold medal game, they could not affect the drama of the game itself. As with any sporting contest, the action could have been one-sided or dull. This was not the case. Describing the game, Bruce Arthur from *The National Post* writes, "The game was played with a desperate ferocity, and at eye-watering speed.... Every puck mattered; every play mattered. Everything mattered." While Arthur's observations are undoubtedly inflected by the game's conclusion, his assessment of the drama is accurate. Throughout the match, the intensity and quality of play was high. With less than thirty seconds left in the third period, the American team scored a goal to tie the game. When the period concluded, there was no winner, and an overtime period was necessary. The first team to score a goal would win the game. With just over 13 minutes left in the overtime period, Canadian player Sidney Crosby shot the puck toward the American goalie. When the "goal" lights flashed, the audience, both inside the stadium and on the festival city streets went wild: they jumped up and down; they screamed; they hugged one another and high-fived. Such celebrations were enacted across the country. For instance, Raveena Aulakh of *The Toronto Star* described the post-game scene in downtown Toronto as follows:

> Downtown streets, virtually empty during the game as Canada played and fans cheered them from sports bars, living rooms and basement dens, overflowed with jubilation as fans in Canadian hockey colours, maple leafs printed on their faces and flags in their hands streamed into Yonge St. ... Traffic slowed to a snail's pace or stopped altogether as motorists honked, cheered and joined in the celebrations.
>
> (Aulakh)

Of course, Canadian sport audiences have long been celebrating live sporting event victories across geographical locations. Critically, however, emerging hockey audience practices have shifted the relations amongst mass and simple audience members.

The men's gold medal hockey game had multiple audiences: the event-audience inside the stadium, the festival audience on the streets of Vancouver, innumerable simple audiences gathered in unique viewing contexts, and the mass audience, the combination of all these audiences. In the twentieth century, these audiences would have been able to imagine each other, but, as noted above, they remained relatively distinct. Smart phone technologies, social media, and newly emerging hockey audience practices re-shaped the relations between audiences during the game. Spectators during the men's 2010 game could and did share text messages, images, audio, and videos with each other in real-time. Individuals also shared real-time messages, images, audio, and video on public and semi-public sites such as Facebook, YouTube, and Twitter. A Twitter search of the hashtag "van2010," for instance, reveals that thousands of people were using their phones to share brief messages and pictures with the public. This informal hashtag search complements official social media data from the Olympics. According to final reports, the IOC's Facebook page attracted 1.5 million fans and 200 million impressions; the official Vancouver 2010 Twitter account had 14, 000 followers, and over 11, 000 photos were shared by 600 photographers on the photo-sharing site Flickr (International Olympic Committee). The content of these sites suggests that audience members were not only recording and responding to the game; they were also recording and responding to each other. Two YouTube compilation videos (JL N), for instance, show dozens of simple audience reactions to Sidney Crosby's goal.

This had two important implications for audience experiences. First, following Schneider's conceptualization of inter(in)animation, the behaviours and gestures of the 2010 hockey audience members prompted a syncopated temporality that was inflected by the genealogy of enactments of past Canadian hockey audiences such as the 1972 Summit Series. By recording the game for potential future posting or viewing, spectators added an additional layer of temporality to their experience. In short, the experience was potentially punctuated by both the past and the future. Second, with the real-time sharing of recordings, members of various audiences (the event audience, the festival audience, the innumerable simple audiences) could, and did, see each other co-temporally, co-orienting toward the game alongside millions of other Canadians. This functioned to heighten the grandeur of the event by increasing the perceived size of the audience. It also amplified the affective dimension of the intersubjective enactments that took place during the game. Canadians were able to see and sometimes hear themselves clapping, cheering, and hugging across geographical space. In doing so, the imagined mass audience became legible to itself through the circulation of text, images, and videos: spectators could, and did, see and hear each other, orienting toward and behaving in relation to the game in real-time.

This is not to suggest that the behaviours or feelings of these spectators were uniformly enacted or experienced. In the early twenty-first century, men's hockey continues to be an exclusive version of Canadian identity that reifies white, able-bodied, neo-liberal, patriarchal logics. Individual responses to the game were necessarily variable, complex, and unknowable. An individual who raucously cheered after Sidney Crosby's goal may have performed their support to mask feelings of alienation or bewilderment. Moreover, many Canadians intentionally did not enact audience practices, choosing, instead, to orient themselves away from the game or to immerse themselves in other activities. For many Canadians, however, the game's mass viewership meant that it was difficult to avoid entirely. This was compounded by the circulation of media reports after the game. Following the match, traditional media outlets such as radio, newspaper, and television reported the size of the audience, described and showed footage of intersubjective enactments, and commented on the felt effects of these enactments. For example, *Vancouver Province* newspaper writers Ken Spencer and Ian Austin suggested that "a connective feeling of national joy took hold of the crowds—a shared emotion many said they'd never felt so strongly." Gary Mason of the Canada-wide newspaper *The Globe and Mail* commented on the mass audience, noting that millions of "Canadians watching were thinking the same thing. The Olympics were over. But the party was just getting started" (Mason). Statistics also played a role in confirming the size of the audience, and it was estimated that 26.5 million people watched some portion of the game (Zelkovich). In addition to these more traditional reports, there was also a flurry of more eccentric ways that intersubjective audience enactments were confirmed, as several cities released water consumption statistics infographics that suggested that people throughout Canadian cities avoided missing the action of the game by not using the washroom (Nusca). Such reports helped secure the game's position in Canada's majoritarian cultural imaginary. This had contradictory effects. As I have previously argued, the celebratory enactments that took place during the men's gold medal match obscured the tragic and insidious elements of the Vancouver Olympic Games (Blair). This included obfuscating the death of Georgian luger Nodar Kumaritashvili and distracting attention from the implementation of the Assistance to Shelter Act, which was widely criticized by civil rights advocate as a veiled attempt to remove Vancouver's homeless population from the streets of downtown Vancouver during the Games (Hyslop; Wintonyk). At the same time, however, for some Canadians, the game produced powerful feelings of community and solidarity, helping to shape positive personal experiences and memories. To this point, between 2010 and 2020, the game was frequently cited as one of the country's "greatest sporting moments" (Battle; Giddens).

Conclusion

Writing in the late twentieth century, Gruneau and Whitson suggested that "the only thing that can be said with any certainty in the case of hockey is that the automatic equation of hockey and 'Canadianness' that existed for much of the postwar era will be far less significant in the future than it has been in the past" (270). In some respects, Gruneau and Whitson's predictions have been realized. The commodification of professional hockey, the predominance of American teams in the NHL, the increased number of international players in the NHL, Canada's changing socio-cultural conditions, and the changing North American sport media landscape have altered the relationship between audiences and hockey in the early twenty-first century, and hockey's place in Canada's cultural imaginary is not quite a forceful as it was at the end of the twentieth century.[7] As the men's gold medal match at the 2010 Olympic

Game evinces, however, hockey's "mystique" has yet to be reduced to mere nostalgia. This is, in part, because of audience performances. As the study of hockey audiences in Canada evinces when audience members act together—when they cheer, jeer, or clap—they manifest a set of experienced, observable, and now recordable, intersubjective behaviours. While individual experiences and enactments are shaped a spectator's unique relation to the sporting action, they are also inflected by their relationship between audience members. In the case of hockey in Canada, these co-performances play a key role in extending the sport's relationship in Canada's cultural imaginary. To this end, the seven Canadian NHL teams each draw an average in-person audience of between 16,000 and 19,000 fans across their 82+ game season (ESPN), the Saturday night television show *Hockey Night in Canada* draws a television viewership that averages 7.5 million per week (Rogers Media "Rogers Media and CBC") and NHL playoffs can draw millions of television viewers (Rogers Media, "Millions." This functions as a critical reminder that audience enactments matter not only because they co-constitute occasions but also because they can bridge the relationship audiences and publics, and in so doing, can maintain and circulate ideas and ideologies across domains.

Notes

1 The description is based on a range of sources including video clips, newspaper descriptions, and my personal experiences in Canada in 2010. For more, see: Aulakh; JL N; Olympics; Olympic Vancouver 2010.
2 For more on events, see: Carlson; Fischer-Lichte, *The Routledge Introduction*; Schechner; Taylor; Turner.
3 For more on theatre audience studies, see; Bennett; Grehan; Harvie; Heim; Kennedy; McAuley; Rancière; Sedgman.
4 For more on participatory theatre audiences, see: Bishop; Harvie; Heim; White.
5 For more on the history of sport in Canada, see: Hall; Kidd; Vennum.
6 For more on hockey in the Canadian cultural imaginary, see: Buma; Gruneau and Whistson *Hockey Night*; Gruneau and Whitson *Artificial Ice*; Lorenz; Melançon, *The Rocket*; Melançon "Writing Maurice Richard"; Oliver; Podnieks Robidoux "Imagining a Canadian Identity"; Robidoux *Stickhandling*.
7 For an in-depth examination of these changes, see: Gruneau and Whitson, 199–301.

References

"Audience, n." *OED Online*, Oxford University Press, March 2022, www.oed.com/view/Entry/13022.
Abercrombie, Nicholas and Brian Longhurst. *Audiences: A Sociological Theory of Performance and Imagination*. Sage, 1998.
Ahmed, Sara. *Queer Phenomenology: Orientations, Objects, Others*. Duke University Press, 2006.
———. *The Cultural Politics of Emotion*. Edinburgh University Press, 2004.
Arthur, Bruce. "We're Left with a Warm Feeling." *National Post*, March 1, 2010.

Austin, Ian. "Golden Ending for Olympics; Hockey Overtime Win Caps Best-Ever Games for Proud Canadian Finish." *The Province*, March 1, 2010. Print.

Aulakh, Raveena. "Rapture on Yonge St. as Fans Celebrate Hockey Gold." *Toronto Star*, February 28, 2010, https://www.thestar.com/news/gta/2010/02/28/rapture_on_yonge_st_as_fans_celebrate_hockey_gold.html. Accessed 1 February 2019.

Auslander, Philip. "Liveness." *Reading Contemporary Performance: Theatricality across Genres*, Meiling Cheng et al., editors, Routledge, 2016, 154, doi:10.4324/9780203103838.

———. *Liveness: Performance in a Mediatized Culture*. Routledge, 1999.

Bennett, Susan. *Theatre Audiences: A Theory of Production and Reception*. Second edition, Routledge, 1997.

Bishop, Claire, editor. *Participation*. Whitechapel, 2006.

Blair, Kelsey. "Hockey Sticks and Heartstrings: The Men's Gold Medal Hockey Game and the Affective Legacy of the 2010 Olympic Games." *Canadian Theatre Review*, vol. 164, no. 164, 2015, pp. 83–8.

Bredtmann, Julia, et al. "Olympic Medals: Does the Past Predict the Future?" *Significance*, vol. 13, no. 3, 2016, pp. 22–5, doi:10.1111/j.1740-9713.2016.00915.x.

Buma, Michael. *Refereeing Identity: The Cultural Work of Canadian Hockey Novels*. McGill-Queen's University Press, 2012.

Health, Canada. "Safety of Cell Phones and Cell Phone Towers." *Government of Canada, Health*, October 14, 2012, https://www.canada.ca/en/health-canada/services/consumer-radiation/safety-cell-phones-cell-phone-towers.html.

Chen, Mel Y. *Animacies: Biopolitics, Racial Mattering, and Queer Affect*. Duke University Press, 2012.

Clough, Patricia Ticineto, et al. *The Affective Turn: Theorizing the Social*. Duke University Press, 2007.

Conner, Lynne and Ebooks Corporation. *Audience Engagement and the Role of Arts Talk in the Digital Era*. Palgrave Macmillan, 2013.

Crawford, Garry. *Consuming Sport: Fans, Sport, and Culture*. Routledge, 2004.

Crego, Robert. *Sports and Games of the 18th and 19th Centuries*. Greenwood Publishing Group, 2003.

Davis, Tracy C. *The Cambridge Companion to Performance Studies*. Cambridge University Press, 2008.

Debord, Guy. *The Society of the Spectacle*. Zone Books, 1994.

Deleuze, Gilles and Felix Guattari. *A Thousand Plateaus: Capitalism and Schizophrenia*. Translated by Brian Massumi. University of Minnesota Press, 1987.

Dickinson, Peter, Kirsty Johnston and Keren Zaiontz. "Mega-Event Cities: Art/Audiences/Aftermaths." *Public*, vol. 27, no. 53, 2016, pp. 5–12.

Dolan, Jill. *Utopia in Performance: Finding Hope at the Theater*. University of Michigan Press, 2005.

ESPN. "NHL Attendance Report," *ESPN.com*, https://www.espn.com/nhl/attendance.

Fischer-Lichte, Erika, et al. *The Routledge Introduction to Theatre and Performance Studies*. English Language, Routledge, Taylor & Francis Group, 2014, doi:10.4324/9780203068731.

Fischer-Lichte, Erika and Saskya Iris Jain. *The Transformative Power of Performance: A New Aesthetics*. Routledge, 2008, doi:10.4324/9780203894989.

Girginov, Vassil, editor. *The Olympics: A Critical Reader*. Routledge, 2010.

Gold, Margaret. "The Olympic Games and Cultural Policy." *Contemporary Theatre Review*, vol. 23, no. 4, Nov. 2013, pp. 598–99. *Taylor and Francis+NEJM*, doi:10.10 80/10486801.2013.839178.

Gregg, Melissa and Gregory J. Seigworth. *The Affect Theory Reader*. Duke University Press, Durham, NC, 2010.

Grehan, Helena. *Performance, Ethics and Spectatorship in a Global Age*. Palgrave Macmillan, 2009.

Gruneau, Richard S. *Class, Sports, and Social Development*. University of Massachusetts Press, 1983.

Gruneau, Richard S. and David Whitson. *Hockey Night in Canada: Sport, Identities and Cultural Politics*. Garamond Press, 1993.

Hall, Ann. *The Girl and the Game: A History of Women's Sport in Canada*. Second edition, University of Toronto Press, 2016.

Harvie, Jen. *Fair Play: Art, Performance and Neoliberalism*. Palgrave Macmillan, 2013.

Harvie, Jen and Keren Zaiontz. "Introduction: The Cultural Politics of London 2012." *Contemporary Theatre Review*, vol. 23, no. 4, Nov. 2013, pp. 476–85. *Taylor and Francis+NEJM*, doi:10.1080/10486801.2013.839174.

Heim, Caroline, and Taylor & Francis eBooks A–Z. *Audience as Performer: The Changing Role of Theatre Audiences in the Twenty-First Century*. Routledge, 2015, doi:10.4324/9781315757568.

Hurley, Erin. editor. *Theatres of Affect*. Playwrights Canada Press, 2014.

———. *National Performance: Representing Quebec from Expo 67 to Céline Dion*. University of Toronto Press, 2011.

———. *Theatre & Feeling*. Palgrave Macmillan, 2010.

Hyslop, Lucy. "Winter Olympics on Slippery Slope after Vancouver Crackdown on Homeless." *The Guardian*, February 3, 2010, https://www.theguardian.com/world/2010/feb/03/vancouver-winter-olympics-homeless-row. Accessed 1 March 2019.

International Olympic Committee. "Final Report of the IOC Coordination Commission: XXI Olympic Winter Games, Vancouver 2010," May, 2011.

JL, N. "Compilation of Canada's Reactions to Men's Hockey Gold Part 1 of 2 (Vancouver 2010) – YouTube." *YouTube*, https://www.youtube.com/watch?v=v-v2A4o47too. Accessed 1 February 2019.

———. "Compilation of Canada's Reactions to Men's Hockey Gold Part 2 of 2 (Vancouver 2010) – YouTube." *YouTube*, https://www.youtube.com/watch?v=Pu-JH2WXJGHI. Accessed 1 February 2019.

Kennedy, Dennis. *The Spectator and the Spectacle: Audiences in Modernity and Postmodernity*. Cambridge University Press, 2009.

———. *The Spectator and the Spectacle: Audiences in Modernity and Postmodernity*. Cambridge University Press, 2009.

Kidd, Bruce. *The Struggle for Canadian Sport*. University of Toronto Press, 2017.

Kreft, Lev. "Sport as a Drama." *Journal of the Philosophy of Sport*, vol. 39, no. 2, Oct. 2012, pp. 219–34. *Taylor and Francis+NEJM*, doi:10.1080/00948705.2012.725898.

Lorenz, Stacy L. "Constructing a Cultural History of Canadian Hockey." *The International Journal of the History of Sport*, vol. 32, no. 17, 2015, pp. 2107–13, doi:10.1080/09523367.2016.1152265.

MacAloon, John J., et al., editors. *Rite, Drama, Festival, Spectacle: Rehearsals toward a Theory of Cultural Performance*. Institute for the Study of Human Issues, 1984.

———. *This Great Symbol: Pierre De Coubertin and the Origins of the Modern Olympic Games*. University of Chicago Press, 1981.

Magnay, Jacquelin. "Winter Olympics 2010: Raw Footage of Nodar Kumaritashvili Death Left Me Shaking—Telegraph." *Telegraph*, 13 February 2010. https://www.telegraph.co.uk/sport/othersports/winter-olympics/7231264/Winter-Olympics-2010-raw-footage-of-Nodar-Kumaritashvili-death-left-me-shaking.html. Accessed 4 May 2016.

Massumi, Brian. *Parables for the Virtual: Movement, Affect, Sensation*. Duke University Press, 2002.

———. "The Autonomy of Affect." *Cultural Critique*, vol. 31, 1995, pp. 83–109.

Phelan, Peggy. *Unmarked: The Politics of Performance*. Routledge, 1996.

Mason, Gary. "A Golden End to Games That Altered Nation." *The Globe and Mail; Toronto, Ont.*, March 1, 2010, p. A.8.

McKinnie, Michael. "Olympian Performance: The Cultural Economics of the Opening Ceremony of London 2012." *Public*, vol. 27, no. 53, 2016, pp. 49–57.

Melançon, Benoît. *The Rocket: A Cultural History of Maurice Richard*. Greystone Books, 2009.

———. "Writing Maurice Richard. High Culture, Popular Culture, Sporting Culture." *Globe*, vol. 9, no. 2, 2006, pp. 109–136.

Messner, Michael A. *Out of Play: Critical Essays on Gender and Sport*. State University of New York Press, 2007.

———. *Power at Play: Sports and the Problem of Masculinity*. Beacon Press, 1992.

Messner, Michael A. and Donald F. Sabo. *Sport, Men, and the Gender Order: Critical Feminist Perspectives*. Human Kinetics Books, 1990.

Nusca, Andrew. "Infographic: Water Consumption in Edmonton, Canada during Olympic Gold Medal Hockey Game." *ZDNet*, https://www.zdnet.com/article/infographic-water-consumption-in-edmonton-canada-during-olympic-gold-medal-hockey-game/. Accessed 31 January 2019.

Olympic Vancouver 2010, "Canada Win Ice Hockey Vold V USA – Highlights – Vancouver 2010 Winter Olympics," YouTube, March 1, 2010, https://www.youtube.com/watch?v=G7DeQbTzPE8.

Olympics. "Canada V USA – Condensed Men's Ice Hockey Final 2010 Throwback," YouTube, February 28, 2019, https://www.youtube.com/watch?v=hun0OG97PHc.

Rand, Silas Tertius, *Legends of the Micmacs*. Wellesley Philological Publications, 1893

Robidoux, Michael A. "Imagining a Canadian Identity through Sport: A Historical Interpretation of Lacrosse and Hockey." *The Journal of American Folklore*, vol. 115, no. 456, 2002, pp. 209–5, doi:10.1353/jaf.2002.0021.

———. *Stickhandling through the Margins: First Nations Hockey in Canada*. University of Toronto Press, 2012.

Roche, Maurice. *Megaevents and Modernity: Olympics and Expos in the Growth of Global Culture*. Routledge, 2002. www-taylorfrancis-com.ezproxy.library.ubc.ca, doi:10.4324/9780203443941.

Roosevelt, Theodore. *Strenuous Life*. Edited by Scott Joplin, Gebbie and company, 1903.

Roger Media. "Rogers Media and CBC Sign New Licensing Agreement for Hockey Night in Canada Broadcasts and Stanley Cup," December 19, 2017, https://about.rogers.com/news-ideas/rogers-media-and-cbc-sign-new-7-year-sub-licensing-agreement-for-hockey-night-in-canada-broadcasts-and-stanley-cup-playoffs/.

Rogers Media. "Millions of Canadians Tuned in to Sportsnet for Return of Live NHL and NBA Action This Weekend," August 4, 2020, https://about.rogers.com/news-ideas/10-7-million-canadians-tuned-in-to-sportsnet-for-return-of-live-nhl-and-nba-action-this-weekend/.
Russell, George Horne, Hockey Match, Victoria Rink, Montreal, QC, composite, 1893, II–101415, McCord Stewart Museum.
Sedgwick, Eve Kosofsky and Adam Frank. *Touching Feeling: Affect, Pedagogy, Performativity*. Duke University Press, 2003.
Spencer, Kent and Ian Austin. "City Throngs Celebrate Hocky Win." *The Vancouver Province*, March 1, 2010.
Schechner, Richard. *Between Theater & Anthropology*. University of Pennsylvania Press, 1985.
———. *Performance Theory*. Routledge, 2004 doi:10.4324/9780203426630.
Schechner, Richard and Sara Brady. *Performance Studies: An Introduction*. Third ed, Routledge, 2013.
Schechner, Richard. *Performance Theory*. Rev. and expanded ed., with A new preface, Routledge, 2003.
Schneider, Rebecca. *Performing Remains: Art and War in Times of Theatrical Reenactment*. Routledge, 2011.
Sinclair, Archibald and William Henry. *Swimming*. Longmans, Green, and Company, 1893.
Sports, and Olympics. *Flashback: Crosby Makes Leap from Superstar to Legend | National Post*. February 28, 2011, https://news.nationalpost.com/sports/olympics/flashback-crosby-makes-leap-from-superstar-to-legend. Accessed 3 February 2018.
Sedgman, Kirsty. *The Reasonable Audience: Theatre Etiquette, Behaviour Policing, and the Live Performance Experience*. 1st ed. 2018.
Spatz, Ben. *What a Body Can Do: Technique as Knowledge, Practice as Research*. Routledge, Taylor & Francis Group, 2015.
Striff, Erin, editor. *Performance Studies*. Palgrave Macmillan, 2003.
Sugden, John Peter and Alan Tomlinson, editors. *Power Games: A Critical Sociology of Sport*. Routledge, 2002.
Vennum, Thomas, et al. *American Indian Lacrosse: Little Brother of War*. Johns Hopkins paperback, Johns Hopkins University Press, 2008.
White, Gareth. *Audience Participation in Theatre: Aesthetics of the Invitation*. Palgrave Macmillan, 2013.
Whitson, David, et al. *Artificial Ice: Hockey, Culture, and Commerce*. Broadview Press, 2006, doi:10.3138/j.ctt2ttwng.
Whitson, David and Richard S. Gruneau. *Artificial Ice: Hockey, Culture, and Commerce*. Broadview Press, 2006, doi:10.3138/j.ctt2ttwng.
Wintonyk, Darcy. "B.C. Introduces Controversial Law on Homelessness | CTV News." *The Guardian*, 3 Feb. 2010, https://bc.ctvnews.ca/b-c-introduces-controversial-homeless-law-1.448858.
Zaiontz, Keren. "On the Streets/within the Stadium: Art for and against the 'System' in Oppositional Responses to London 2012." *Contemporary Theatre Review*, vol. 23, no. 4, Nov. 2013, pp. 502–18. *Taylor and Francis+NEJM*, doi:10.1080/10486801.2013.839183.
Zeisler, Laurel. *Historical Dictionary of Ice Hockey*. Scarecrow Press, 2012.
Zelkovich, Chris. "Gold-Medal Hockey Game Watched by Record 16.6 Million | The Star." *The Toronto Star*, 1 Mar. 2010,

4

SEQUENCES OF ACTION ACROSS GENRES

Injury Mini-Dramas and American Football

During a regular season road game against the Dallas Cowboys in 2015, Seattle Seahawks' player Ricardo Lockette was tackled and immediately knocked unconscious.[1] As his body lay limp on the field, a conventional sequence of behaviours unfolded: players backed away from the scene, the audience quieted, health and safety personnel rushed onto the field to tend to the injured player, and the audience applauded when Lockette was carted off the field. The sequence of action that follows serious sporting injuries—the stoppage of play, the removal of the injured player from the player space, the final applause—is not embedded in any single sporting activity or event. Rather, it is a conventional set of behaviours that crosses multiple activities and events and involves a range of possible grouping of participants including athletes, audience members, and health and safety personnel. In this way, the sequence is akin to discrete strings of action in other genres of performance such as pre-show announcements, intermissions, or curtain calls. How should we understand conventional sequences of action that cut across activities and events within performance genres? What gets carried out during such sequences?

To review, I contend that performance events are occasions that are demarcated from everyday life and where multiple participant groups enact sequences of behaviours that are stitched together by rules, conventions, laws, and traditions (by configurations). In performance events, performers who enact specialized skills—actors, musicians, athletes etc.—and audience members are commonly recognized participant groupings, but there are, in fact, different roles within participant groupings and there can also be multiple, distinct, groups of participants. In terms of roles, an activity configuration may include several different categories of performer. In sport, roles include athletes, coaches, referees, officials, and judges. In other performance genres, roles include orchestra conductors, contest judges, and masters of ceremonies. The behaviours of these performers are patterned by located activity configurations. In elite, international, badminton, for example, the behaviours of linespersons are shaped by the Laws of Badminton, which dictate that linespersons should remain seated and also offer instructions for how to signal that a shuttlecock has landed inbounds by holding one arm out in front of the hand open, palm facing toward the ground (Badminton World Federation) Whereas, in western classical orchestral music, the conductor is conventionally located in front of the orchestra, on a pedestal, with their back facing the audience. In terms of participant groupings, there are persons whose behaviours might be related to activity or audience configurations but whose enactments are not directly patterned by either. For instance, venue ushers facilitate and sometimes enforce audience-seating arrangements; they play a key role in performance events, but their behaviours are not directly addressed by the rules, laws, conventions, or traditions of the activity, and their actions do not directly impact the sporting action. Nor are ushers audience members, as their gestures and movements are shaped by a distinct set of responsibilities. As with performers and audience members, the behaviours of different participant groupings are simultaneously patterned by areas of technique and configurations. For instance, an usher's practice is patterned by areas of everyday technique (walking, pointing, etc.) and by a configuration that shapes the ebb and flow of action and rest during a sporting event. Similarly, mascot's tumbling routine is at once structured by the areas of technique of dance and gymnastics and by a configuration that orients the mascot towards the audience.

While performance studies scholars often acknowledge the existence of participants who are neither performers nor audience members, the patterning of behaviour of such persons is rarely closely examined. Analyzing the gestures and movements of such participants recognizes the central role that labourers, facilitators, technicians, health and safety staff, pageantry performers, and volunteers might play in performance events. It also helps illuminate conventional sequences of action that cut across activities within a performance genre. To explore further, I introduce the concept of sporting injury mini-dramas, by which I mean the conventional behaviours that follow serious injuries in sports. As I outline in the first section of this chapter, while this sequence of action has a practical function in sporting events (usually, to tend to the athletes), it also has a range of philosophical, affective, and social implications. To illustrate the effects of these implications in the performance genre of sport, I turn to gridiron football. Outlining the development of gridiron football in the United States in the twentieth century, I demonstrate how victory and injury became mutually constitutive elements of the game's logics. Building from this, I investigate two twenty-first-century National Football League (NFL) games involving the professional team the Seattle Seahawks. I aim to illuminate how injury mini-dramas contribute to the affective scene of contemporary professional gridiron football in the United States, and in so doing, to show how sequences of action involving multiple groups of participants can shape contemporary sport performances.

Conventional Sequences of Action: Injury and Mini-dramas

In his semiotic analysis of theatrical curtain calls, Revermann argues that curtain calls are "liminal mini-dramas in their own right, with their own dynamics, scripted-ness, and distinct modes of semiotization" (194). The concept of liminal mini-dramas helpfully names conventional sequences of action that take place during performance events. There are obviously differences between different types of mini-dramas but pre-show announcements, curtain calls, the singing of national anthems, and sporting injury dramas also share key features: they involve behaviours of multiple groups of participants, they feature conventional sequences of behaviours, and these sequences of behaviour are commonly incorporated across a range of performance events within and across genres. They also all exist in or near the threshold between the performance activity and everyday life. Announcements and the singing of national anthems, for example, tend to precede the aesthetic performance in theatre, dance, music, and circus or the contest-action in sports. Importantly, mini-dramas serve a range of functions within performance occasions. Some of these functions are practical; announcements, for example, often involve etiquette reminders (such as turning of technology) or safety information. Other functions are psychological or philosophical. Writing of curtain calls, Revermann notes: "The predominant feature of the curtain call phase from an audience perspective is clearly the notion of release. The curtain call marks the end of a prolonged period of imprisonment, both emotional and physical" (197).

The conventional sequence of behaviours during a sporting injury are as follows. First, an athlete gets injured or suspects that they are injured. For the drama of a sporting injury to take place, the athlete's injury stops or impedes their ability to perform specialized and everyday practice (such as walking off the court or field or swimming to shore). In sports that take place on land (as opposed to in the water or in the air), the athlete typically falls to the ground. If it is an upper-body injury, however, the athlete may remain upright. Second, the sporting action is paused. In sporting activities where competitors share the playing space, this pause usually halts the sporting action mid-play; in sporting activities where competitors compete consecutively, such as weightlifting or gymnastics, or in sports where athletes do not compete in the same space, such as swimming or sprinting, this pause may take place between races. Third, this pause conventionally stills and quiets performers, audience members, and other participants. Fourth, two opposing sets of movements take place on the playing space. Most performers will retreat from the injured player while a few select performers and performance participants will move toward the athlete.

The roles of the people who move toward the injured athlete vary by level and can include teammates, other athletes, coaches, trainers, first aid attendants, or emergency personnel. Fifth, the other participants look on as these individuals tend to the injured athlete. Sixth, alone or with help, the injured athlete exits the playing space. Seventh, all performance event participants applaud. The applause concludes the injury drama and the sporting action continues.[2]

To understand the function of this liminal mini-drama, one must first understand the potential disruptions caused by serious injuries. When an athlete gets seriously injured, it potentially unsettles a sporting event in two key ways. First, in occasions where an injury prevents an athlete from exiting the playing space, serious injuries delay or pause the sporting action. Second, even though sporting activities do not involve dramatis personae or fictional worlds, the behaviours and actions that take place during a sporting activity are still separated from everyday life. Meanings, associations, and narratives can be layered onto athletes, but serious injuries are not representational. As such, when athletes get seriously injured, the other event participants encounter an authentically harmed human body. The affective process cued by this encounter varies by individual; some spectators may be fascinated while others might be uneasy. It also varies by participant group; health and safety personnel, for instance, are likely to respond differently than audience members. Critically, however, all participants know that the harmed human body exceeds the temporal and spatial boundaries of the event: when the game ends, the athlete will still be injured. Combined with the stoppage in play, this potentially disrupts the event.

The liminal mini-drama practically, psychologically, and philosophically contains such potential disruptions. Practically, the drama of sporting injuries provides a conventional sequence of behaviours for performance participants to enact. This sequence has two concrete purposes. The first is to tend to the athlete, and the second is to remove the athlete from the playing space. The trained attention, space, and equipment needed to evaluate and treat a serious injury are usually outside of the playing or event space, so removing an athlete from the playing space is the first step of getting them to the support they need. It also takes the athlete out of a public setting so that they can experience the injury in private. Transporting an athlete out of the playing space is not, however, only motivated by support and care. As noted above, seriously injured athletes are obstacles on the playing space, and to ensure fair competition, they need to be removed so that the action can continue. Psychologically, these conventional behaviours help organize the experience of the encounter with an injured body, potentially transforming a situation into a mini-drama. In *Cruel Optimism*, Lauren Berlant argues that cruel genres "provide an affective expectation of the experience of watching something unfold, whether that thing is in life or in art" (6). She suggests that situations are genres of emergent happenings where "a state of things in which something that will perhaps matter is unfolding amid the usual activity of life" (4), and further claims that a situation "forces one to take notice, to become *interested* in potential changes to ordinariness. When a situation unfolds, people try to maintain themselves in it until they figure out how to adjust" (195). The sequencing of action rapidly shifts an instance of injury from a situation, an emergent happening where people must figure out how to adjust, into an organized mini-drama, where roles, behaviours, and expectations are clear. So, while the athlete's health status might remain uncertain, the broad elements of the action are stable.

Philosophically, the liminal mini-drama temporarily transforms participant roles. The liminal mini-drama re-organizes participants for the duration of the conventional sequence of action, and participants such as coaches, trainers, or medical staff may become performers in the mini-drama while the roles of other participants, such as security guards, may shift in relation to these role transformations. Critically, most performance event participants are transformed into sporting injury audience members. Consequently, the relations between individuals temporarily shifts and individuals who were members of distinct performance participant groups become allied with one another through their shared relation to the injury action. As with other audience practices, this does not mean that all participants feel, express, or behave uniformly. One audience member might turn away from the action while another might watch the scene intently. If they remain in the stadium and behave in relation to the injury scene, however, they potentially become injury-drama audience members.

The conclusion of this mini-drama knits the practical, psychological, and philosophical effects of the sequence of action together and functions to manage its affective effects. Having been relatively still and quiet for the duration of their encounter with a harmed body, the applause that concludes the sporting injury mini-drama functions similarly to the applause of a curtain call: it provides the audience with physical and emotional release. At the same time, by clapping, each mini-drama spectator member fulfils their role as an audience member by recognizing the action through the gesture, and, crucially, they do so alongside all the other mini-drama audience members. This intersubjective enactment helps the injury audience complete their role in the injury scene, which effectively rewards individuals for their occasion-appropriate participation in the injury drama. This helps to fold feelings not contained by the injury drama back into the performance event, facilitating a return to the sporting action. As the case of injuries in contemporary American football evinces, this process can have significant socio-political effects.

Injury, Masculinity, and the Genealogy of American Football

To understand the significance of mini-injury dramas in contemporary football, it is first necessary to contextualize the relationship between injury, masculinity, and the development of American football in the twentieth

FIGURE 4.1 Harvard versus McGill football match, Montreal, QC, composite photograph, 1875 painted by Henry Sandham and photographed by William Notman Studio.

century. Indigenous peoples in North America played team ball games for centuries before Europeans arrived in their territories.[3] The emergence of gridiron football, however, was strongly influenced by the genealogy of contests that developed from mob or folk football contests in western Europe in the middle-ages. Mob football games took place between two villages, involved an unlimited number of players, and included few rules. The objective of mob football games was simple: advance an object into the opponent's territory. Alongside the division of competitors into two teams, this objective influenced the development of soccer, rugby, and gridiron football, all of which stabilized into recognizable and distinct sports in the nineteenth century. Unlike soccer and rugby, both of which were primarily standardized in Britain, gridiron football emerged in the United States, and more specifically on north-eastern college campuses in the United States in the late nineteenth century. As a consequence, football in the United States in the late nineteenth century was primarily played and developed by middle to upper-class, able-bodied, white men.

As with other team sports such as soccer and basketball, the rules of football evolved rapidly in the late nineteenth and early twentieth century. Since the 1910s, however, the game's general shape has remained relatively stable. Football is a full-contact sport that involves two teams of eleven players competing to advance the ball into the other team's end-zone or scoring area. The offensive team has a limited number of attempts or "downs" (four in American football; three in Canadian football) to advance the ball ten yards; if they fail to do so, the other team, formerly the defensive side, is given possession of the ball and becomes the offensive side. Teams score points by throwing or running the ball into the other team's end zone, or by kicking the ball through a set of posts in the end zone. The game resembles other contemporary full-contact ball games such as rugby, Australian rules football, and hurling, but has several distinct rules. Of these rules, those that pertain to physical contact are particularly important for understanding the game's internal logics.

In football, full-body physical contact falls into two main categories: blocking and tackling. In rugby, the off-side rule decrees that a player cannot gain advantage from being in front of the ball. A player who is "offside", meaning in front of the ball, cannot receive a pass, enter a scrum, play the ball, move toward the ball, or obstruct a player from the other team. Consequently, blocking is forbidden in rugby. In football, blocking takes place when one player uses their body to obstruct or impede another player's movement; tackling, on the other hand, involves holding another player or bringing that player to the ground. It is illegal to tackle a player without the ball, but, as the rules clearly state, "a player of either team may block (obstruct or impede) an opponent at any time" (Goodell 46). By stepping onto the field of play during a full-contact football game, then, players implicitly accept the possibility that full-body, person-to-person, contact could occur at any time. Moreover, when they catch, carry, or hold the ball during play, they surrender their right to personal space and consent to being tackled. This consent is inextricably linked to the game's objective: in football, the aim is to advance the ball across the field. Alongside the objective of football contests, these rules help stitch together one of football's underlying logics: possession and advancement of the ball is more important than the safety of any individual human body. Following this logic, injury and serious bodily harm have been conventional components of the game since the early twentieth century.

This is evinced by a controversy regarding the high incidence of player injuries and deaths during the 1905 collegiate football season. *The Chicago Tribune* reported that 19 football players died during the 1905 season (McCracken). While this was double the average of football-related deaths from the previous five years, the statistics reported indicate that a total of 45 players died during football games in the 1899–1904 seasons, suggesting that while football deaths were uncommon, they were not unheard of during this period. Moreover, the article reports 137 serious football injuries in the 1905 season. These injuries included 19 broken collarbones and shoulders, 31 broken legs, 19 fractures of "some portion of the head", nine broken arms, three broken ribs, three spinal injuries, and three concussions of the brain ("Football Year's"). As the article notes, this list only accounts for "accidents out of the ordinary" ("Football Year's), so it is likely that there were many more injuries that were considered "ordinary". The fatalities and serious injuries prompted a meeting between President Theodore Roosevelt and university representatives from Harvard, Yale, and Princeton, during which Roosevelt supposedly encouraged the representatives to reform the rules (Zezima). The meeting led to a nation-wide gathering of 68 university and college administrators (Oriard). During this meeting, the National Collegiate Athletics Association (NCAA) was formed and rules were amended. Despite these changes, however, football has remained a full-contact physical contest involving a high-degree of personal risk.

As has been detailed by sport sociologists and historians, football's brutality, strategic elements, and internal logic made the game perfectly suited for associations with nationalism and masculinity in the United States (Oriard; Crawford; Burstyn; Gems). To these ends, while women were actively advocating for, and often obtaining, increased access to sport participation in the early twentieth century, football's emphasis on full-body physical contact discouraged female participation and essentially made football all-male for much of the twentieth century. This made football an ideal site for the cultivation of a certain kind of American masculinity (white, middle-class, able-bodied). Indeed, two years before he was elected as President of the United States, Theodore Roosevelt delivered a speech titled "The Strenuous Life" in Chicago, Illinois. The speech began with a personal call for men to undertake the strenuous life, "the life of toil and effort, of labor and strife" (Roosevelt 21) and concluded by expanding the concept of the strenuous life to the fate of the American nation, declaring that it was "only through strife, through hard and dangerous endeavor, that [America could] ultimately win the goal of true national greatness" (Roosevelt 21). Roosevelt extended this link to athletics in a speech at Harvard Union in 1907:

> We cannot afford to turn out of college men who shrink from physical effort or from a little physical pain. In any republic, courage is a prime necessity for the average citizen if he is to be a good citizen; and he needs physical courage no less than moral courage ... Athletics are good, especially in their rougher forms, because they tend to develop such courage. They are good also because they encourage a good democratic spirit. (qtd. in Umphlett, 87)

Roosevelt does not name football specifically, but it is easy to see how football's roughness and the implied risk of personal injury were ideal for the cultivation of such values.

In the mid and late twentieth century, the culture of American football expanded to include professional football, which existed prior to World War II but had previously struggled to gain popularity. During this period, the general configuration of football remained relatively stable, meaning that while there were minor rule changes, the general rules of the game were similar across time. One of the key elements of football transformed, however: the game's relationship with capitalism. The NFL was always a profit-seeking organization, but in the latter half of the twentieth century, the intensity of the commodification of the NFL was unparalleled in American sports.[4] As Thomas Oates and Zach Furness argue:

> Though competing leagues, such as Major League Baseball, the National Basketball Association, the Barclay's Premier League, and Formula One, stake a claim to some of the most visible, influential, and successful brands in the contemporary sports marketplace, they cannot compete with the incredible concentration of wealth and power in the NFL. (4)

In combination with the mediatization of football through television—and later Internet—broadcast, the massive wealth generated by the commodification of the NFL torques the internal logics of the game. In contemporary professional football players are expected to sacrifice their bodies in service of collective success *and* for the audience who pays to consume the performances upon which these sacrifices are predicated.

The Seattle Seahawks, Injury Dramas, and the NFL's Affective Scene in the Twenty-First Century

Affect theorists such as Sara Ahmed and Lauren Berlant use the term "promise" to conceptualize the relation between expectations, attachments, and experiences. Whether it's the promise of happiness (Ahmed) or "the good life" (Berlant), these theorists contend that people orient themselves toward phenomena based on their expectation of what they believe those phenomena will provide for them. As Ahmed argues, "To think the genealogy of expectations is to think about promises and how they point us somewhere, which is 'the where' from which we expect so much" (Happiness 29). For instance, because the affective scene of a football game involves the drama of sport, the spectator expects that they will encounter a contest that involves the enactment of specialized skills performed by individuals who compete as themselves. Encounters with this drama may produce a range of emotional responses (thrill, excitement, suspense, etc.), but the meeting of the expectation (the promise of drama) tends to produce a single affective intensity: the pleasure of assurance. This pleasure "does not have to feel good viscerally" (Berlant Female 14); rather, it is a result of "the self-confirmation one receives by repeating the dynamics of an affective scene" (Berlant Female 14). Promises and the pleasure of assurance they can prompt help explain how the drama of sport can simultaneously invoke negative emotions (disappointment with the outcome, anger with the referees, etc.) and positive affective intensities.

In the contemporary NFL, American masculinity, community celebration, and spectacle are so tightly bound to professional football that they contribute to the matrix of promises that shape each game's affective scene. This scene is, then, packaged and sold to audience members. These promises include expectations regarding performance occasion (a sporting event), activity (football, a contest involving two teams of eleven players competing against one another to advance a ball over a pre-determined territory), practice (specialized skills structured by the areas of technique of athletics and the configuration of football), performers (highly trained professional men), participant groups (athletes, audience members, pageantry performers, broadcasters, vendors, venue staff, security guards, etc.), spectacle (grandeur provided by size of in-stadium and mass audience, pageantry performers, and technology), and the logics and meanings embedded in each of these elements (bodily sacrifice for sporting success and the audience; intersubjective audience celebration linked to on-field enactments of exceptional instances of male bodily practice). Injuries are not an explicit element of this matrix of promises. As a close analysis of two incidents involving the Seattle Seahawks reveals, however, the sequences of action that follow instances of serious injury are a critical, if implicit, element of the NFL's affective scene and the product that the NFL sells to its audience.

The Seattle Seahawks joined the NFL in 1976, and, as with other franchises, the team invokes a range of local expectations based on factors such as the team's history, its win-loss record, its star players, its relation to other professional sports, and its place in the city's civic imaginary. For the Seahawks, the most important of these local expectations is that spectators get to participate in the distinct culture of the Seahawks fandom. The team—like most NFL franchises—draws large numbers of spectators. The Seattle Seahawks home game attendance percentage—meaning the percentage of seats filled—has consistently ranked in the top 15 in the NFL since 2012, and in the 2021–2022 NFL season, the team has an average attendance of approximately 547,000 at regular season home games. These spectators contribute to Seattle Seahawks' spectator culture. As the only NFL franchise in the Pacific Northwest, the Seattle Seahawks draw spectators from Oregon, Idaho, Alaska, and British Columbia (across the border in Canada), and the franchise actively cultivates a meaningful relationship with spectators and fans. To this end, the Seattle spectators have been dubbed the "12th Man", a phrase that is meant to indicate that the audience plays such an important role during games that the audience is like an extra player ("The 12s"). The spectator culture of Seattle Seahawks games gestures to the investments, attachments, and expectations that individual spectators may have with the Seattle Seahawks' team. The term "fan" is now used to describe spectator-performance or consumer-producer/product relations across a range of cultural domains, but it was first used to describe "keen and regular" ("fan, n.2") spectators at American baseball games in the nineteenth century. In the last one hundred years, the term "fan" has come to denote "a keen follower" or "an enthusiast" ("fan, n.2"). In other words, "fan" denotes a person who has a strong, meaningful, relation with an individual and an object, person, or persons. Inflected by a person's history, memories, knowledges, and emotional attachments, individual relations between a fan and the Seahawks are unique. This does not mean that every individual in the stadium is a fan (even if they were, this would only constitute one dimension of their relation to the game). Rather, the visible and audible presence of Seahawks' fans in the stadium during a match amplifies the promise that spectators will have the opportunity to participate in a group enactment of American masculinity and community building.

The incident now known as the "Beast Quake" exemplifies the intense affective experiences that accompany the fulfilment of the NFL's matrix of promises. In 2011, The Seahawks played against the New Orleans Saints during a wild card game. The NFL is divided into two conferences which are separated into four divisions, and each division is comprised of four teams. The four division champions from each conference earn a playoff berth. In addition, each conference has two "wild card" berths; these two berths are given to the remaining teams with the best record. In the first round of playoffs, the top two seeds from each conference are given a "by" into the divisional round, while the remaining teams play in wild-card games. The Saints were the defending Super Bowl champions, but their 11–5 regular season record was not strong enough to claim a divisional title. The Seahawks, on the other hand, had won the divisional title, but did so with a losing record of 7–9. During the regular season, the Saints had beaten the Seahawks 34–19. In other words, despite their division title, the Seahawks were the underdog and it was widely speculated that the Saints would easily win the wild-card game.

The situation of a single-elimination playoff game heightens the stakes of the game and, consequently, increases the intensity of the affective scene. In the case of the Seahawks' 2011 wild-card game, the Seahawks had built a four-point lead by the game's fourth quarter. With four minutes and twenty seconds left to play in the game, the Seahawks received the ball. On the first play, Marshawn Lynch—a star running back with the nickname "beast mode", a moniker meant to capture his powerful playing style and his ability to break tackles—was stopped at the Seahawks' 33-yard line with 3 minutes and 38 seconds left in the game. This put the Seahawks in a precarious position. In the NFL, teams get four downs to advance the ball toward the other opponent's goal line. When they fail to do so, the ball is turned over to the other team. If the Seahawks were to turn the ball over—through an interception or through downs—the Saints would have plenty of time to score a touchdown, which would give them the lead. On the first play, Lynch was easily stopped. On the second play, however, Lynch broke free with the ball.

Wearing bulky padding and thick helmets, football players at the line of scrimmage blend into a group of bodies, but when an individual player separates himself from the pack, his individual achievements are highlighted. In these moments, the player embodies the ideal American masculine body: the strong, skilled man who takes a personal risk and, in doing so, achieves individual and collective success. After puncturing the line of scrimmage, Lynch ran down the field. Saint players attempted to tackle him, but Lynch was able to shirk the contact or evade being tackled. As he ran down the field, the spectators' cheers got louder and louder. Lynch's teammates and Saints players ran to catch him. The Seahawks players blocked the Saints, protecting Lynch from further contact. Approximately sixteen seconds after the play began, Lynch completed a 67-yard touchdown run. As he crossed into the end-zone, the fans reacted with aggrandized, dynamic expressions of support and cheer. As is customary when a player scores a touchdown, they clapped and cheered. They also made large, dynamic gestures such as arm waving, jumping up and down, and stomping their feet. Based on video footage of the run ("'Beast Quake'"), the enactments can best be described as expressions of ecstasy and joy. According to one report, the audience's celebratory enactments were powerful enough to register on a nearby seismograph, meaning it was possible to claim that the response to Lynch's run had caused a minor earthquake (Vidale). With this information, Lynch's run became known within football and sporting circles as "the Beast Quake" (Heifetz).

These expressions index the heightened emotional responses that follow the fulfilment of the NFL's matrix of promises. By attending this Seahawks' wild-card game, audience members got to watch a sporting contest where two teams of eleven highly skilled, professional players competed to enact specialized practice during an activity underpinned by individual sacrifice in service of collective success and associated with American masculinity; in doing so, each spectator became a member of the broader audience participant group during an event where their intersubjective enactments were supported, encouraged, and heightened by the presence of pageantry performers and the broadcast configuration that expanded the mass audience to a national-scale. When Lynch successfully crossed the goal-line, these promises coalesced, cueing several overlapping affective processes that were underpinned by the pleasure of the assurance of the affective scene for Seahawks' fans. As with the men's 2010 Olympic gold medal hockey match discussed in the previous chapter, this pleasure was affirmed through the circulation of video, images, and news reports following the game.

Crucially, however, these ecstatic celebratory behaviours represent only one side of the NFL's affective scene, and a separate game injury to another Seahawks player, Ricardo Lockette, evinces the more insidious elements of the NFL's affective scene. Unlike Lynch, Lockette was not a star NFL player. An undrafted free agent, he became an active member of the Seahawks' roster in the 2011–2012 season; he was not, however, a significant contributor to the team and was released in the pre-season of 2012. After brief stints with San Francisco and Chicago, he returned to the Seahawks in October 2013 and remained with the team for two years. During a regular season road game against the Dallas Cowboys, Lockette was on the field. In a play away from the ball, Lockette was hit by Dallas Cowboys' safety Jeff Heath and knocked unconscious. In this moment, the NFL's matrix of promises appeared to break down; this, however, was not the case. Rather, these actions indexed the beginning of the sporting injury mini-drama.

In the case of Lockette's injury, no less than seven trainers and emergency personnel walked onto the field during the injury drama, and their presence uncloaked one of the obscured NFL configurations: the medical configuration. Sporting events frequently include various health and safety personnel, but not all sports require the same volume or kinds of staff. Recreational and amateur sporting events often have persons trained in basic first aid, but usually no dedicated medical responders; elite and professional sports, on the other hand, may include multiple first aid persons and medical staff. Moreover, the injuries arising in car races differ significantly from those that take place in swim competitions; consequently, the kinds of health and safety attendants vary by sport. While trainers and physiotherapists now populate the sidelines of NFL games, emergency personnel and medical staff tend to be situated on the far edges of the field or remain behind-the-scenes, in rooms underneath the stadium seating. When athletes require support from medical staff, they frequently exit the playing space and disappear into these behind-the-scenes locations. In cases of serious injury, however, these personnel must come to the athletes. In doing so, the medical configuration is uncloaked, and it is revealed that numerous, highly trained medical staff and emergency personnel are always present and equipped to tend to serious bodily harm.

During the action of the liminal-mini-drama, these staff become performers whose practice is simultaneously structured by the areas of technique of emergency first aid and by the configuration of the liminal mini-drama wherein the purpose of the drama is to both tend to the athlete and remove the injured player from the playing space. In Lockette's case, the staff worked quickly and a mini truck drove onto the field, in the event that Lockette needed to be transported away. Less than ten minutes after appearing on the field, trainers and staff secured Lockette onto a spine board and lifted him onto the truck. As the truck drove off the field, the audience applauded and Lockette raised his fist to recognize their applause. In doing so, all the participants participated in the closure of the injury drama, helping to fold any residual emotions back into the overall event. Moments later, the game continued, and the health personnel disappeared behind the scenes. Or, more accurately, they disappeared until they were needed again.

Behaviours enacted by non-emergency personnel during Lockette's injury index the operation of the NFL's affective machinery. As the medical staff tended to Lockette on the field, players, coaches, and spectators stilled their motions, brought their limbs close to their bodies, and waited quietly for the action of the injury drama to unfold. These gestures, the opposite of those performed during the "Beast Quake", appeared to index feelings of discomfort or unease. Critically, however, the queasy feelings that the injury drama audience members' behaviours appeared to index did not undermine the NFL's affective scene. In fact, the potential discomfort produced by NFL injury dramas is one of the constitutive elements of the promise of the league's affective scene. Nicholas Ridout suggests that the circulation of "queasy" emotions such as shame and embarrassment during theatrical performance is constitutive of the situation of contemporary western theatre. Arguing that theatre "conceives itself as an apparatus for the production of affect by means of representation" (168), he contends that theatre's most powerful affects are "obtained at precisely those moments when the machinery appears to break down" (168).

Since the stabilization of football as a distinct sport in the early twentieth century, all the participants in complex football events implicitly consent to and participate in the game's underlying logics. This includes individual sacrifice for collective success and the risk of bodily harm. Following this, one of the expectations of watching the drama of an NFL football game is that one will watch individuals choose to risk the safety of their bodies in order to contribute to the team's collective victory. Instances of injury function to authenticate this risk: players can and do suffer bodily harm by partaking in football activities. This, in turn, amplifies the stakes of the NFL's affective scene, wherein enactments are simultaneously underpinned by the potential for success and the potential for serious harm. As such, while spectators may experience feelings of worry, unease, or discomfort during injury dramas, the pleasure of assurance also underpins such situations: in watching a player get seriously hurt, the spectator's expectations about the game are confirmed. This effectively authenticates the risks of NFL football games, thereby supporting the NFL's affective scene and the NFL brand. And, crucially, the sequence of action of the sporting injury mini-drama help fold experiences of discomfort back into the event itself: by participating in the drama, participants facilitate a return to sporting action. This not only evinces the significance of injury-mini-dramas in sport, it also suggests the role that conventional behavioural sequences within genres can play in shaping what gets carried during contemporary performances. As the player demographics of the contemporary NFL suggests, the implications of the effects of mini-dramas extend beyond the context of any single performance.

Mini-Dramas, Race, and Resistance in the Contemporary NFL

Sporting injury-mini drams—and their affective consequences—are particularly insidious in the context of shifting demographics of the NFL in the last one hundred years. Between 1920 and 1933, there were 13 Black players in the NFL (Ross, 21). This number decreased to zero in 1934 (Ross, 49). Though there are no confirmed reports, the shift is widely attributed to a "gentleman's agreement" initiated by George Preston Marshall, owner of the Boston Red Skins.[5] It is said that Marshall convinced other owners not to hire Black players (Ros 49–79; Smith 259), so while there was no official rule in place, between 1934 and 1945, the NFL was all-white. This changed when Kenny Washington and Woody Strode were hired by the Rams in 1946; the unofficial "colour line" was broken.[6] As a consequence of a range of intersecting factors, including the civil rights movement, the recruiting practices of the NFL's competitor, the American Football League, and interventions by president-elect John F. Kennedy, the number of Black players in the NFL steadily increased after 1960 (Oriard, *Brand* 210), and since the early 1990s, Black players have consistently comprised over fifty per cent of NFL players. To this point, the Institute for Diversity and Ethics in Sport, reported that 58% per cent of NFL players identified as Black or African-American in 2021 (Lapchick 8). As such, unlike the 1920s, where the performance of American masculinity on the NFL football field was primarily enacted by white men, in the early twenty-first century, it is primarily enacted by Black men, and it is, therefore, predominantly Black men who are expected to sacrifice their bodies for both the team and the audience.[7]

As noted above, over fifty per cent of professional football players in the NFL identify as Black or African American. In relationship with injury statistics, this has significant consequences. For example, in 2015–2016 NFL season—the season when Ricardo Lockette was injured—the total number of reported, number of concussions, ACL, and MCL injuries in the NFL was 494 (National Football League). The accuracy of these categories is difficult to ascertain, as "suspected concussions" or borderline cases may not be reported by teams. Moreover, because the NFL's report does not include other serious injuries, such as broken bones, spinal injuries, or non-knee-related tendon and muscle tears, the total number of injuries that take place during an NFL season is significantly higher than the report suggests. Critically, the racial demographics of the contemporary NFL mean that the personal consequences of these injuries are overwhelmingly experienced by Black male athletes. To this end, in Week 8 of the 2015–2016 NFL season—the week of Ricardo Lockette's Injury—one hundred percent (11/11) of Seattle Seahawks players on the injury list were Black or African American. Unsettling the oppressive structures and ideologies that flow within the contemporary NFL is not the responsibility of Black male athletes, however. As Kimberly George suggests, the work and knowledge of Black male athletes are already frequently disavowed by the majoritarian logics underpinning the league (264). Rather, it is the responsibility of all participants to unsettle the NFL's powerful affective machinery and to imagine new modes of participation. Intriguingly, injury-mini-dramas, perhaps, offer a site of potential resistance.

As conventional sequences of action, mini-dramas are malleable, and their behaviours can be adjusted, changed, or refused. Pre-show announcements can be integrated into the first scene of a theatrical show; intermissions during circus shows can be omitted; audience members can refuse to applaud in curtain calls. In sports, where rules play a major role in the stitching together of behaviours, it can be difficult to imagine resisting activity parameters, as behaviours that break rules are frequently immediately penalized. Liminal mini-dramas, however, are often outside of the contests themselves, and their action sequences are often stitched together through convention or tradition. As such, mini-dramas may present an opportunity for transformation. In fact, in the contemporary NFL, one of the most widely acknowledged instances of protest took place in the mini-drama of the pre-game anthem. NFL games are preceded by the playing of the American national anthem. During a pre-season game in 2016–2017, 49ers quarterback Colin Kaepernick kneeled during the singing of the national anthem in protest of police violence and the treatment of Black Americans and people of colour in the United States. In a post-game interview in August 2016, Kaepernick explained the motivation for his protests.

> I am not going to stand up to show pride in a flag for a country that oppresses black people and people of color. To me, this is bigger than football and it would be selfish on my part to look the other way. There are bodies in the street and people getting paid leave and getting away with murder. (Boren)

In kneeling during the national anthem, Kaepernick refused one of the logics of the mini-drama (to acknowledge and honour nation). His protest prompted nation-wide debate that was taken up by a range of members of society from casual sports' fans to military veterans to the President-Elect.[8] His actions also spurred a wider protest movement amongst athletes across sports, levels, and national contexts from youth gridiron football (Gleeson) to professional (Lacques) to international football (Bushnell) This suggests the potential of mini-dramas as sites of subversion. What would it mean to refuse the sporting injury mini-drama? What if players didn't return to the field after serious injuries? What if audiences left the auditorium? What if serious injuries did not simply pause football games but stopped them? Such provocations offer a lever for re-imagining mini-drama performances and also signal the importance of examining the full range of sequences of action that take place during sporting events.

Notes

1 Description of the event compiled from: Kelly; Montano.
2 It is important to note that the conventional sequence of action vary by sport. In soccer, for example, if a player from either team recognizes a serious injury, they conventionally kick the ball out of bounds to stop play. Following the injury, the team throwing the ball in will conventionally give it back.
3 The genealogy of football is constructed from a range of sources. See: Mark Bernstein; Crawford; Curry and Dunning; Gems; Oriard *King Football*; Oriard *Reading Football*; PFRA Research.
4 For a history of the commodification of the NFL, see: Oriard, *Brand NFL*
5 See: Ross, 49–79; Smith, 259.
6 See: Crawford, 20; Ross 49–79.
7 This shift has been rigorously outlined and analyzed by football scholars. See: Oriard; Ross; Brown; Gems.
8 For more on the range of commentators on Colin Kaepernick's kneel, see: Graham; Lowary.

References

"2021 Injury Report", NFL, https://www.nfl.com/injuries/league/2015/REG8.
National Football League. "2015 Injury Data". *NFL.com*, 07 Feb, 2022, https://www.nfl.com/playerhealthandsafety/health-and-wellness/injury-data/injury-data.
"NFL – Attendance 2012–2021" NFL Football Attendance – National Football League – ESPN". *ESPN.Com*, http://www.espn.com/nfl/attendance.
Ahmed, Sara. "Happy Objects". *The Affect Theory Reader*, edited by Melissa Gregg and Gregory J. Seigworth, Duke University Press, 2010, pp. 29–51.
———. *The Promise of Happiness*. Duke University Press, 2010, doi:10.1215/9780822392781.
Badminton World Federation. "Instructions to Technical Officials: Section 4.1.1" Laws of Badminton *BWF Badminton.com*, 22 May 2022, https://corporate.bwfbadminton.com/statutes/#1513733461252-a16ae05d-1fc9
"Beast Quake". *Wikipedia*, 20 Nov. 2018. *Wikipedia*, https://en.wikipedia.org/w/index.php?title=Beast_Quake&oldid=869772075.
Berlant, Lauren Gail. *Cruel Optimism*. Duke University Press, 2011.
Bernstein, Mark F. *Football: The Ivy League Origins of an American Obsession*. University of Pennsylvania Press, 2001.
Burstyn, Varda, et al. *The Rites of Men: Manhood, Politics, and the Culture of Sport*. University of Toronto Press, 1999, doi:10.3138/j.ctt2tts8t. 2002, pp. 145–56.
Bushnell, Henry. "USWNT, other soccer teams kneel before Olympic openers to protest racism" *Yahoo Sports.com*, 21 July, 2021, https://ca.sports.yahoo.com/news/olympics-soccer-players-kneel-uswnt-090330888.html
Boren, Cindy. "A Timeline of Colin Kaepernick's Protests against Police Brutality, Four Years after They Began", *Washington Post*, August 26, 2020, https://www.washingtonpost.com/sports/2020/06/01/colin-kaepernick-kneeling-history/.

Crawford, Garry. *Consuming Sport: Fans, Sport, and Culture*. Routledge, 2004.
Crawford, Russ. "Football's History and Reach." *Football, Culture, Power*, edited by David J. Leonard, Kimberly B. George, and Wade Davis, Routledge, 2017, doi:10.4324/9781315685014.
Crego, Robert. *Sports and Games of the 18th and 19th Centuries*. Greenwood Publishing Group, 2003.
Crepeau, Richard C. "Le Football: A History of American Football in France". *Journal of American History*, vol. 104, no. 2, 2017, pp. 565–66, doi:10.1093/jahist/jax295.
Curry, Graham and Eric Dunning. "The Folk Antecedents of Modern Football". *Association Football: A Study in Figurational Sociology*, Routledge, Taylor & Francis Group, 2015, doi:10.4324/9781315738369.
Demas, Lane. *Integrating the Gridiron: Black Civil Rights and American College Football*. Rutgers University Press, 2010.
Dolan, Jill. *Utopia in Performance: Finding Hope at the Theater*. University of Michigan Press, 2005.
Dunning, Eric. *Fighting Fans: Football Hooliganism as a World Phenomenon*. University College Dublin Press, 2002.
Dunning, Eric et al. *Sport Histories: Figurational Studies in the Development of Modern Sports*. Routledge, 2004, doi:10.4324/9780203497432.
Dunning, Eric and Patrick Murphy, et al. *The Roots of Football Hooliganism: An Historical and Sociological Study*. Routledge & Kegan Paul, 1988.
Dyck, Noel, editor. *Games, Sports and Cultures*. Berg, 2000.
Dyck, Noel and Eduardo P. Archetti. *Sport, Dance, and Embodied Identities*. 1st ed., Berg, 2003.
"fan, n.2". *OED Online*, Oxford University Press, March 2022, www.oed.com/view/Entry/68000.
Gems, Gerald R. *For Pride, Profit, and Patriarchy: Football and the Incorporation of American Cultural Values*. Scarecrow Press, 2000.
George, Kim. "A Feminist Football Fan: On the Psychic Life of Spectatorship". *Football, Culture and Power*, edited by David J. Leonard, Kimberly B. George, and Wade Davis, Routledge, 2017, pp. 256–274, doi:10.4324/9781315685014.
Giulianotti, Richard, et al. *Football, Violence and Social Identity*. Routledge, 1994.
Gleeson, Scott. "Team of 8-year-olds kneels during national anthem to support St. Louis demonstrators," *USA Today*, 20 September, 2017, https://www.usatoday.com/story/sports/2017/09/20/team-8-year-olds-kneels-national-anthem-support-st-louis-demonstrators/684292001/
Goodell, Roger. *2018 Official Playing Rules of the National Football League*. National Football League, 2018.
Graham, Bryan Armen. "Donald Trump Blasts NFL Anthem Protestors: "Get That Son of a Bitch Off the Field." The Guardian, 23 September 2017, https://www.theguardian.com/sport/2017/sep/22/donald-trump-nfl-national-anthem-protests.
Haerens, Margaret. *The NFL National Anthem Protests*. ABC-CLIO, 2018.
Heifetz, Danny. "How Marshawn Lynch's 'Beast Quake' Run Changed the Seahawks Forever, *The Ringer"*, 7 Jan, 2021, https://www.theringer.com/nfl/2021/1/7/22217035/beast-quake-marshawn-lynch-10-year-anniversary-seattle-seahawks-saints
Hopkins, Matt and James Treadwell, editors. *Football Hooliganism, Fan Behaviour and Crime: Contemporary Issues*. Palgrave Macmillan, 2014.

Horowitz, Helen Lefkowitz. *Campus Life: Undergraduate Cultures from the End of the Eighteenth Century to the Present.* 1st ed., A.A. Knopf, 1987.
Kelly, Luke. "Ricardo Lockette Injury – YouTube". *YouTube,* https://www.youtube.com/watch?v=7BEx1BqTlhI. Accessed 1 February 2019.
Kennedy, Dennis. *The Spectator and the Spectacle: Audiences in Modernity and Postmodernity.* Cambridge University Press, 2009.
———. *The Spectator and the Spectacle: Audiences in Modernity and Postmodernity.* Cambridge University Press, 2009.
Kimmel, Michael S. *Manhood in America: A Cultural History.* Fourth, Oxford University Press, 2018.
King, Richard. "Look Away: On the Racial, Sexual, and Cultural Politics of the NFL". *Football, Culture and Power,* edited by David J. Leonard, Kimberly B. George, and Wade Davis, Routledge, 2017, pp. 27–43, doi:10.4324/9781315685014.
Kreft, Lev. "Sport as a Drama". *Journal of the Philosophy of Sport,* vol. 39, no. 2, Oct. 2012, pp. 219–34. *Taylor and Francis+NEJM,* doi:10.1080/00948705.2012.725898.
Lacques, Gabe. "'We're still on this fight': Yankees' Giancarlo Stanton, Aaron Hicks kneel during national anthem." *USA Today,* July 26, 2020, https://www.usatoday.com/story/sports/mlb/yankees/2020/07/25/giancarlo-stanton-aaron-hicks-yankees-kneel-national-anthem/5512427002/
Lowary, Jake. "What do veterans think about kneeling during the anthem? Views are diverse." *The Tennessean,* 28 September, 2017, https://www.tennessean.com/story/news/politics/2017/09/28/kneeling-anthem-veterans-opinions-nfl/709488001/
McCracken, Henry M. "Football Year's Death Harvest". *Chicago Tribune,* 26 Nov. 1901, p. 1.
McIntosh, Peter C. *Fair Play: Ethics in Sport and Education.* Heinemann, 1979.
Mez, Jesse, et al. "Clinicopathological Evaluation of Chronic Traumatic Encephalopathy in Players of American Football". *JAMA,* vol. 318, no. 4, 2017, pp. 360–70, doi:10.1001/jama.2017.8334.
Montano, Ryan. "Ricardo Lockette Injury – YouTube". *YouTube,* November 1, 2015, https://www.youtube.com/watch?v=7BEx1BqTlhI.
Murphy, Patrick J., et al. *The Roots of Football Hooliganism: An Historical and Sociological Study,* Taylor and Francis, 2014, doi:10.4324/9781315772875.
Oates, Thomas Patrick, et al. *The NFL: Critical and Cultural Perspectives.* Temple University Press, 2014.
Oriard, Michael. *Brand NFL: Making and Selling America's Favorite Sport.* University of North Carolina Press, 2007.
———. *King Football: Sport and Spectacle in the Golden Age of Radio and Newsreels, Movies and Magazines, the Weekly and the Daily Press.* University of North Carolina Press, 2001.
———. *Reading Football: How the Popular Press Created an American Spectacle.* University of North Carolina Press, 1993.
"Pershing Picks Type for National Army: Thinking Men with Individuality, Healthy and Well Disciplined, Are Needed". *New York Times,* August 8, 1917, p. 2.
PFRA Research. "Camp and His Followers: American Football 1876–1889". *Profootballresearchers.com,* http://www.profootballresearchers.org/articles/Camp_And_Followers.pdf. Accessed 1 February 2019.
Revermann, Martin. "The Semiotics of Curtain Calls". *Semiotica: Journal of the International Association for Semiotic Studies/Revue De l'Association Internationale De Sémiotique,* vol. 168, no. 1–4, 2008, p. 191, doi:10.1515/SEM.2008.010.

Richardson, Dean. "Player Violence: An Essay on Torts and Sports". *Stanford Law & Policy Review*, vol. 15, no. 1, 2004, p. 133.

Riess, Steven A. *Sport in Industrial America, 1850–1920*. Harlan Davidson, 1995.

Ridout, Nicholas P. *Stage Fright, Animals, and Other Theatrical Problems*. Cambridge University Press, Cambridge, 2006

Ross, Charles Kenyatta. *Outside the Lines: African Americans and the Integration of the National Football League*. New York University Press, 1999.

Rinehart, Robert E. *Players All: Performances in Contemporary Sport*. Indiana University Press, 1998.

Rozik, Eli. *The Roots of Theatre: Rethinking Ritual and Other Theories of Origin*. University of Iowa Press, 2002.

Saigal, Rajiv. "The Long-Term Effects of Repetitive Mild Head Injuries in Sports". *Neurosurgery*, vol. 75, no. 4, 2014, p. 155.

Sandham, Henry, *Harvard versus McGill football match, Montreal, QC*, composite photograph, 1875, II-21493, McCord Stewart Museum.

Smith, Thomas G. "Outside the Pale: The Exclusion of Blacks from the National Football League, 1934–1946". *Journal of Sport History*, vol. 15, no. 3, 1988, pp. 255–81.

Spaaij, R. "Men Like Us, Boys Like Them: Violence, Masculinity, and Collective Identity in Football Hooliganism". *Journal of Sport and Social Issues*, vol. 32, no. 4, 2008, pp. 369–92, doi:10.1177/0193723508324082.

———. "Sports Crowd Violence: An Interdisciplinary Synthesis". *Aggression and Violent Behavior*, vol. 19, no. 2, 2014, pp. 146–55, doi:10.1016/j.avb.2014.02.002.

"The 12s, Seattle Seahawks Fans | Seattle Seahawks – Seahawks.Com". *Seahawks*, https://www.seahawks.com/fans/the-12s/. Accessed 1 February 2019.

Vennum, Thomas, et al. *American Indian Lacrosse: Little Brother of War*. Johns Hopkins paperback, Johns Hopkins University Press, 2008.

Vidale, John. "One Year Ago, Seattle Seahawks 12th Man Earthquake". *Pacific Northwest Seismic Network*, https://pnsn.org//blog/post. Accessed 28 February 2019.

"Weekly Team Injuries throughout the Season"*NFL.Com*. http://www.nfl.com/injuries?week=1. Accessed 3 March 2019.

Wyche, Steve. "Colin Kaepernick Explains Why He Sat during National Anthem". *NFL*, 27 Aug. 2016, http://www.nfl.com/news/story/0ap3000000691077/article/colin-kaepernick-explains-why-he-sat-during-national-anthem. Accessed 3 March 2019.

5
GESTURAL MARKS IN SPORT PERFORMANCE, THE GENEALOGY OF THE BUTTERFLY, AND THE REFUGEE OLYMPIC TEAM

A swimmer steps onto a starting block for a 100-metre butterfly competition.[1] Wearing a white swim cap, she gently shakes her arms and slowly crouches into the starting position. Alongside four other swimmers, she waits. The starter announces, "Take your marks". The swimmer contracts her muscles in anticipation. Beep!

The swimmer bounds off the block and into the water. Elbows locked, hands clasped above her head, the swimmer undulates her legs underwater for several seconds. When she finally surfaces, she performs the butterfly stroke. By the last 25 metres of the race, the swimmer leads. Her stroke remains fluid and consistent, and when she touches the wall, she is the clear winner. The crowd in the pool cheers, but the swimmer does not smile or raise her hands in triumph. It is the first heat of the preliminary round of competition, and her time will not be fast enough to advance to the next round. Despite this, international media outlets widely circulate a report of her race and describe the swimmer's performance as a "symbolic victory" (White 2016).

This swimmer was Syrian refugee Yusra Mardini.

In 2015, Mardini used her competitive swimming skills to tow an inflatable dingy filled with 18 other refugees from Turkey to Greece. A year later, she competed in the 100-metre butterfly and the 100-metre freestyle at the 2016 Olympics under The Refugee Team Flag. Bolstered by the IOC's promotional efforts and a VISA commercial featuring Mardini, her story received international media attention. In this chapter, I draw together the key ideas introduced in the previous chapters to unpack the complex web of performances embedded in Mardini's Olympic participation and to illuminate the

DOI: 10.4324/9781003275879-6

density of the meanings and histories activated by contemporary sport performances. In the first half of the chapter, I demonstrate how the genealogy of the butterfly stoke intersects with the activity configuration of competitive swimming and the meaningful relations in the performance genre of sport. Placing this genealogy in conversation with Carrie Noland's concept of "gestural marks—physical or embodied indicators of gender such as the way one stands or throws a ball—I examine the meanings embedded in the butterfly in the twenty-first century. To demonstrate the significance of the gestural mark in contemporary sport performances, I return to Mardini's butterfly performance at the 2016 Olympic Games in Rio. Drawing together the multiple threads of Mardini's performance at the Games, I argue that her multiple performances at the Games contributed to an officially sanctioned narrative about perseverance and inspiration that supported the ideology of Olympism but functioned to obscure the nation-state logics that undergird Olympic participation.

The Emergence of the Butterfly Stroke

On a summer day in 1936 in Berlin, seven swimmers—Tetsuo Hamuro of Japan, Erwin Sietas of Germany, Reizo Koike of Japan, John Higgins of the United States, Saburo Ito of Japan, Jochen Balke of Germany, and Teófilo Yldefonso of the Philippines—crouch on outdoor blocks of the Berlin Olympic Swim Stadium. Behind the swimmers, a man in a suit slowly raises his arms above his head. He pauses.

"Bang!"

The starting gun fires, and the swimmers bound forward, diving into the water headfirst.[2] One by one, they surface and swim in a straight line in their respective lanes. All the swimmers use the breaststroke kick to propel them, but their arm motions differ. Some swimmers use the traditional breaststroke arm motions while others enact what a twenty-first century-observer would recognize as the butterfly arm stroke. In the stands, spectators and coaches cheer to encourage the swimmers. Two minutes, forty-one seconds, and five milliseconds later, Tetsuo Hamuro touches the pool wall, completing his fourth and final lap. He takes a deep breath and dunks his head into the water while he waits for the other swimmers to finish. Moments later, the results are announced: Hamuro has won the race.

To understand why not all the competitors used the same arm stroke, it is necessary to situate the emergence of the butterfly stroke in relation the genealogy of swimming technique. From Ancient Egypt to third century Polynesia to seventeenth century Japan, the area of technique of swimming has structured human practices of moving through water in a range of locations, cultures, and time periods.[3] In Europe prior to the nineteenth century, the popularity of swimming practice ebbed and flowed, in part due to the belief that water contributed to the spread of the plague. Importantly, when individuals did swim in Europe before the 1800s, the primary purpose of their practice was usually to stay afloat in water, for either recreational or survival purposes. The emergence of the sport of swimming in the 1800s popularized a new purpose that patterned swimming practice: speed. The general activity configuration of the sport of swimming—competitive swimming—started to form in the 1800s. This emergence is attributed to the sport's popularity in England. Alongside the proliferation of public municipal bath houses, made possible by the Baths and Washhouses Act in 1846, English people enjoyed recreational swimming throughout the nineteenth century (Love "An Overview" 571). Bolstered by Mathew Webb's 1875 crossing of the English Channel, by the 1890s, there was considerable interest in competitive swimming in England (Love "An Overview" 578). But the growth of competitive swimming was not limited to England. By the end of the nineteenth century, Austria, France, Hungary, New Zealand, and the United States had national swim associations (FINA). The creation of these associations, the establishment of international competitions such as the first European championships, and the inclusion of four swimming events—the 100-metre freestyle; the 500-metre freestyle; the 1200-metre freestyle; and the Sailors 100-metre freestyle—at the first modern Olympic Games in 1896 were all important events in the development of competitive swimming ("Athens 1896")). In addition, in 1908, the Fédération International de Natation (FINA) was formed and the same year, the swim competition at the Olympics was hosted in a pool for the first time. These two developments—the formation of FINA and the 1908 Olympic Games programme—played a major role in the standardization and codification of the rules of competitive swimming and also standardized the conditions in which these events took place (in pools of a set length).

The development of competitive swimming is bound to the conventions of one branch within the performance genre of sport: competitive sport. "Competitive sport" does not describe a specific level or kind of sport; for example, instances of competitive sport can be identified at a range of levels of sport, including youth, top-tier recreational, inter-collegiate, amateur, or professional. Rather, competitive sport refers to practices, activities, and events (and by extension the individuals, institutions, federations, and industries that participate in and organize them) that share a common manipulation of sporting activity configurations. In competitive sports, the shape of activity configurations is torqued so that the significance of competition is heightened. At its most pronounced, this shifts the purpose of the activity from competition to winning. This distinction is subtle. While competition implies the ranking of performers, it does not necessarily suggest that winning is the most important aspect of the ranking. I can participate in a competition with the aim of comparing myself to other performers without believing that a low ranking is failure. In competitive sports, the aim is not only to be ranked; it is to win. This inflects the formation of competitive sports, wherein practice is structured not only by the potentials and constraints of an activity configuration but also by a heightened desire to emerge victorious in relation to others. Importantly, "other" can refer to another competitor or competitors, another version of oneself, or an imagined other, such as an historical figure. In a competitive swim race, for example, I do not simply swim against others to see how I rank in comparison; I swim against others, against previous versions of myself, against all other individuals swimming at my level (if I am an elite athlete), and against all other individuals who have ever and will ever swim (especially if I am an elite world champion-level athlete seeking a world record).

The competitive dimension of international, elite, swimming contests was significant because it influenced experimentation with swimming technique and practice. In the early twentieth century, the general technique of the breaststroke involved a frog kick with the legs and a double, mirrored, arm stroke. One of the key principles of the stroke—which has remained a touchstone in the development of competitive breaststroke through the twentieth and twenty-first centuries—is the concept of the horizontal plane, wherein a swimmer's arms, legs, and torso must remain in the "horizontal plane", meaning parallel to the bottom of the pool. In the 1920s, swimmers began to experiment with the breaststroke arm motion with the aim of increasing their overall breaststroke speed. While historians sometimes attribute the butterfly arm-stroke to a single individual—Australian, Sydney Cavill; German, Eric Rademacher; or American, Henry Myers—it is more accurate to say that, around 1930, competitive swimmers were actively playing with new areas of technique.[4] The double-over-arm-stroke—where the swimmer simultaneously lifts both arms out of the water during the recovery portion of the stroke—emerged as a result of this experimentation. Explaining the difficulty of the butterfly arm stroke in 1936, G. Clifford Larcom, Jr., a writer for Esquire, wrote, "Most swimmers haven't the strength to carry it for over a hundred yards" (79). Despite its difficulty, the stroke was considerably more efficient and powerful than breaststroke's traditional arm movements, and it did not technical break the horizontal plane rule. As such, many competitive swimmers adopted the butterfly arm stroke with the frog kick during breaststroke events. This explains why the swimmers in the 1936 Olympic breaststroke competition featured swimmers using a range of arm motions: the formation of the breaststroke was in flux, resulting in a moment of instability in the practice of breaststroke swimming.

Initially, it appeared that the butterfly arm stroke might supersede the traditional breaststroke recovery, marking a major moment in the genealogy of the breaststroke. This, however, was not the case. Pioneered by American swimmer Jack Sieg and his coach David Armbruster, the dolphin kick—the undulation of the legs to emulate a fish's tail—also emerged in the mid-1930s (Colwin *Breakthrough* 30–31). However, it took twenty years until the dolphin kick and the butterfly arm stroke were combined. This was not because the dolphin kick lacked efficiency or power. Nor were the dolphin kick and double-arm-recovery kept separate because they were incongruous; as anyone who attempts both iterations of the stroke will quickly discover, the dolphin kick is a far more intuitive movement with the double-arm-recovery than the breaststroke kick. Rather, the dolphin kick was not combined with the butterfly arm stroke because it broke the rules for the horizontal plane rule for the breaststroke kick (Colwin *Breakthrough*, 31). From the mid-1930s to the 1950s, swimmers continued to experiment with the stroke, and in non-FINA sanctioned competitions, butterfly races were frequently included in a meet's programme. As a result of its growing popularity, FINA finally recognized the butterfly—with double-arm-out-of-water-recovery and dolphin kick—as an independent stroke in 1954, and the first Olympic butterfly race took place at the 1956 Summer Olympics in Melbourne, Australia ("Melbourne/Stockholm"). The recognition of the butterfly stroke effectively standardized the four major strokes as freestyle, backstroke, breaststroke, and butterfly, and since the emergence of the butterfly, no other major strokes have developed in international competitive swimming.

The Gestural Mark of the Butterfly or Why the Genealogy of the Butterfly Stroke Matters

While the lack of historical materials that directly reference swimming technique in ancient times makes it difficult to know with any degree of certainty, the butterfly stroke appears to be unique to the twentieth century, and unlike the front crawl, backstroke, breaststroke, side stroke, frog stroke, or doggie paddle, the butterfly is a consequence of the activity of competitive swimming, an activity that is an effect of the rise of competitive sport within the larger performance genre of sport. The effects of this emergence are subtle but significant. The result of experimentation by skilled performers in highly controlled aquatic conditions (swimming pools), the butterfly arm stroke is a specialized branch of technique that is considerably more technically and physically demanding than other strokes; to execute the double-arm recovery—to get both arms and the face out of the water—requires shoulder flexibility and strength, good arm stroke technique, a powerful dolphin kick, precise timing between the arm stroke and the dolphin kicks, and, if a swimmer wishes to perform the stroke continuously, sufficient cardiovascular capacity. These elements make the stroke ill-suited for open water settings. In a river, a lake, or an ocean, external factors such as wind or current add a virtually untenable level of difficulty for non-elite swimmers to perform the stroke for long distances.

The difficulty and non-transferability of the butterfly stroke has important implications for the meanings the stroke produces. In her reading of Judith Butler's work on gender and performativity, Carrie Noland queries Butler's expression of "marks of gender" and argues that the difference between "the visible mark of gender, such as wearing lipstick, and the gestural mark of gender, such as throwing without aim, are utterly different entities" (177). Noland suggests that the distinction between different kinds of marks are not adequately parsed out in Butler's works. Building from this, she argues that gestural marks are critical for producing "a more nuanced account of the en-gendering of the body, of its modes of social legibility, and … of the multiple ways in which resistance to culturally dominant modes of subjectivation occurs (177). Whereas Noland applies the concept of gestural mark to the study of gender, I am interested in the gestural mark and its relation to specialized areas of technique.

More specifically, I am interested in gestural mark of the butterfly stroke in the early twenty-first century. As a result of the difficulty of learning and executing the stroke and its impractical use in open water, the butterfly is one of the final skills taught in recreational swimming programs, and in some cases, it is not taught at all. In Austria and Germany, for example, the major learn-to-swim programs—Arbeitsgemeinschaft Österreichisches Wasserrettungswesen and Schwimmabzeichen—each have four levels (Wasserrettungswesen). To receive the highest level, swimmers do not need to perform the butterfly. The Red Cross swimming program, which is used in both the United States and Canada, also does not teach the butterfly (Red Cross 2019). There are, then, three main avenues by which an individual might learn the butterfly stroke: by taking advanced swimming lessons; by joining a competitive swim club; or by engaging in individual learning, either with a coach or through instructional materials. While there are certainly some people who learn the butterfly stroke through individual learning, most people learn the butterfly technique through swim lessons or by joining a competitive swim club. As such, within the context of swimming, the butterfly stroke is a gestural mark that makes training, and more specifically advanced or competitive training, socially legible.

Significantly, the gestural mark of the butterfly is often socio-economically inflected. To learn the butterfly, swimmers must be able to afford to register for multiple courses to reach the advanced classes where the butterfly is taught. For example, where I grew up, in the suburb of North Vancouver, the "I Can Swim" program is used, meaning that a swimmer must complete four courses, priced at approximately $50–$75 each, before the butterfly stroke is taught ("Find a Program"). In regions that do not use swim curricula that include the butterfly, such as the Red Cross programs taught in Vancouver—the urban centre just 30 minutes away from North Vancouver—swimmers must join a swim club to learn the butterfly, and the cost of joining a swim club is drastically higher than the cost of swim lessons. At the point of writing, it costs approximately 950 dollars to join the "fitness group", the lowest level of the city's largest swim club, The Vancouver Dolphins (Canadian Dolphin Swim Club 2019). In addition to financial cost, any swimmer who wants to learn the butterfly must be able to commit the time to training, making it a financial and personal investment that not everyone can afford. The socio-economic inflection of the gestural mark of the butterfly resonates with Pierre Bourdieu's theorization of the relationship between sport and class.

Bourdieu argues that a person's habitus, meaning their embodied dispositions toward the world as informed by their encounters with social structures, influences their relation to sport, and, more specifically, that class plays a major role in directing people toward or away from sport participation and spectatorship. Tracing the emergence of new areas of technique in relation to performance genre builds on Pierre Bourdieu's (1984) theorizations by offering an approach that helps identify the social stratification that takes place within areas of technique and acknowledges the emergent and complex processes that influence this stratification. Certainly, the details of any elite, competitive, swimmer's enactment of freestyle-, back-, or breast-stroke might make their training apparently to other swimmers or onlookers. Critically, however, the social legibility of their training is located in the details of their enactments such as their streamline position or the precision of their arm stroke. In the case of the butterfly, the social legibility of specialized training is located in the stroke itself. Put simply, whereas a specific enactment of freestyle may be inflected by a series of detailed gestural marks that suggest specialized training and socio-economic conditions, the butterfly stroke is a gestural mark that implies specialized training and the socio-economic conditions that specialized training necessitates. Yusra Mardini's performance of the butterfly at the 2016 Summer Olympic Games in Rio illustrates the significance of the gestural mark of the butterfly in contemporary performance.

Yusra Mardini and the Butterfly Stroke at the 2016 Olympic Games

Yusra Mardini's participation in the 2016 Olympic Games marked a complex web of performances and effects, and the gestural mark of the butterfly was an important thread in one strand of this web. World Fairs and Olympic Games are what Maurice Roche calls "mega-events", meaning "largescale cultural (including commercial and sporting) events which have a dramatic character, mass popular appeal and international significance" (1). From their emergence in the nineteenth and twentieth centuries, these events were underpinned by nation-state logics. As Roche explains:

> Mega-events contributed to the development and promulgation among mass publics of notions of nation (national collective identity), nationality (membership or inclusion in the nation's tradition and destiny), and

citizenship (the formal statuses, obligations and rights of participation associated with nationality) ... they also provided apparently 'international' stages and arenas for the display of current versions and ideals of international world order. (198)

Today, the Olympic Games are the largest and most prestigious multi-sport mega-events in the world, and they continue to be important hubs for the reification of nation-state logics and current ideals of the international world order. The contemporary refugee crisis unsettles this logic as it relates to the Olympic Movement. According to the UN Refugee Agency, there are currently 68.5 million forcibly displaced people in the world, and 25.4 million of these people are refugee ("Figures at a Glance"). Until 2015, none of these 25.4 million people were eligible to compete at the Olympic Games. In 2016, this changed. In March 2016, the IOC officially announced the creation of the "Team of Refugee Olympic Athletes", now known as "the Refugee Olympic Team", or the ROT. In the press release, IOC President, Thomas Bach, noted that ROT athletes would "be welcomed to the Olympics Games with the Olympic flag and with the Olympic anthem" ("Team of Refugee Olympic") and emphasized that one of the primary procedural aims for the team was to ensure that athletes would receive the same treatment as their peers and would participate in the welcoming and closing ceremonies, be housed alongside other teams, be provided with uniforms, and be subject to doping testing ("Team of Refugee Olympic"). At the time of the announcement, 43 athletes had been identified for possible team selection. Selection criteria included "sporting level, official refugee status verified by the United Nations, and personal situation and background" ("Refugee Olympic Team to Shine"). By June 2016, 10 athletes had been selected for the 2016 Summer ROT. Of these athletes, only one, Popole Misenga, a male judo athlete originally from the Democratic Republic of the Congo and hosted by Brazil, advanced past the first round of competition, but it was Mardini who garnered the most international media attention. Analyzing Mardini's biography in relation to the gestural mark of the butterfly helps explicate why this was the case.

"Olympic" simultaneously names a series of international sporting festivals and a major global brand, and the relationship between the Olympic brand and the sporting competitions that comprise its festival are critical for contextualizing Mardini's participation in the 2016 Olympic swimming competition. Conceived by Olympic founder Pierre de Coubertin, Olympism is an ideology that links Olympic sports to education and humanitarian values. The first four "fundamental principles" of the most recent Olympic Charter aptly capture the contemporary character of Olympism and help situate the ROT within the context of the Olympics:

1. Olympism is a philosophy of life, exalting and combining in a balanced whole the qualities of body, will and mind ...

2. The goal of Olympism is to place sport at the service of the harmonious development of humankind, with a view to promoting a peaceful society concerned with the preservation of human dignity.
3. The Olympic Movement is the concerted, organised, universal and permanent action, carried out under the supreme authority of the IOC, of all individuals and entities who are inspired by the values of Olympism. It covers the five continents. It reaches its peak with the bringing together of the world's athletes at the great sports festival, the Olympic Games …
4. The practice of sport is a human right. Every individual must have the possibility of practising sport, without discrimination of any kind and in the Olympic spirit, which requires mutual understanding with a spirit of friendship, solidarity and fair play. ("Olympic Charter in Force" 13–14)

From policy documents and qualification infrastructures to branding materials, these principles permeate the organization of the Olympics, and in the case of the ROT and Yusra Mardini, they played a key role in influencing the official narrative advanced by the IOC.

Olympic festivals draw both large volumes of on-site audience members and huge international mass audiences. The Summer Olympics in Rio, for example, sold six million tickets; digital and television broadcast of the Olympics added up to almost 350,000 hours and these hours were shown on more than 500 TV channels and 250 digital platforms; the official IOC website recorded over 26 million visits and their social media posts received more than four billion impressions, meaning views ("Rio 2016 sets records"). From the outset, official press materials and media releases emphasized the symbolic value of the refugee athletes' participation in the Games. In the official team selection announcement, for example, IOC President Thomas Bach suggested that athletes competing under the Olympic banner would function as a "symbol of hope for all the refugees in our world" ("Refugee Olympic Team to shine"). To shape, or perhaps one might say to direct, the stories about specific athletes, the IOC released short biographies, videos, and high-resolution images for each athlete, emphasizing the inspirational aspects of the athletes' journeys to the Olympics.

Mardini's skills as a highly trained swimmer are critical element of her biography. A competitive swimmer from a young age, Mardini grew up near Damascus and represented Syria in four events at the 2012 FINA Short-Course Swimming Championships (25m) when she was twelve years old. Following the destruction of her family home during the Syrian civil war, Mardini and her sister Sarah decided to leave Syria in 2015. They made it to Turkey where, alongside eighteen other people, they intended to cross the Aegean Sea into Greece. During the journey, the boat's motor stopped working. Mardini, her sister, and two other people who could swim got into the water and pushed/towed the boat, and the people inside of it, for more than three hours. Eventually, the boat reached the shores of Lesbos. Mardini's swimming skills had literally saved her life and the lives of the other people in the boat. Following the incident, Mardini and her sister travelled to Germany, where she eventually settled. Throughout 2015 and 2016, Mardini trained with a swim coach in Berlin, and, alongside the other athletes, she was officially selected to the ROT team in June 2016 and she was scheduled to participate in the 100-metre freestyle and 100-metre butterfly events by FINA and the IOC. 3. As I outline below, the International Swimming Federation (FINA) has a complex system for Olympic qualification, and it is important to note that Mardini's race times would not have been fast enough to qualify for the Olympics if it were not for the creation of the ROT. This does not detract from her skills or performance; her swimming in 2016 was elite. It is, however, important for contextualizing her participation in the Games.

The general practice of swimming, as performed during Mardini's journey from Syria to Germany, and Mardini's performance as a competitive swimmer in the context of the Olympics. This offered an ideal rhetorical link for the ideals of Olympism. In her ghost-written autobiography, titled *Butterfly* Mardini describes how this link was noted even before the ROT was selected. Describing a conversation with her coach, Sven, she writes:

> "It's weird that they only want to talk to me," I say to Sven. "What about the other refugee athletes the IOC mentioned as being in the running [for the ROT]? The Congolese guy, the Iranian woman?"
>
> "I'm not sure the journalists have found them," says Sven. "You speak English. And you're Syrian, too. Lots of reporters want to talk about the war. On top of that, there's your amazing story."
>
> "Which story?" I say.
>
> "The boat story, silly," he says.
>
> "Oh that," I say. "But we told that story already to those reporters last year. Why does anyone want to hear it again?"
>
> Sven shakes his head.
>
> "I don't think it works like that," he says. (241–2)

Once she was officially selected for the ROT, the story was bolstered by the fact that Mardini would perform the freestyle, the same stroke she used to push the boat in the Aegean Sea, to train for and compete in the Olympics. Critically, however, while written promotional materials primarily focussed on the link between Mardini's performance of the freestyle in both the Aegean Sea and at the Olympic Games, the IOC's photos and videos emphasized her performance of the butterfly.

The gestural mark of the butterfly is integral for understanding these visual materials. IOC press materials—which are expressly created for circulation to official media outlets—repeatedly noted that, prior to the war in Syria, Mardini was a competitive athlete who represented her country at international competitions and official IOC promotional photos and videos highlighted Mardini's performance of the butterfly. In the IOC video, the first shot of Mardini swimming is of her doing the butterfly and all of the high-resolution IOC action shots of Mardini feature the stroke ("Refugee Olympic Team"). On the one hand, these images are logical, as Mardini was set to swim in the 100-metre butterfly event, and the video also features Mardini performing the freestyle, the other stroke she was scheduled to enact during the Games. On the other hand, the butterfly is also prominently featured in the visual press materials. Of the 33 photos in the IOC ROT gallery, six photos feature Mardini alone, and three of these six photos show her performing an element of the butterfly. There are four feature photos of the other ROT swimmer, Rami Anis (also a refugee from Syria), and only one of these shows Anis enacting a stroke in the pool. Whether intentional or not, one of the effects of the video and these images is that the gestural mark of the butterfly functioned to make Mardini's training socially legible and, by consequence, the socio-economic status that such training would necessitate. This was critical in the socio-political context of 2016 Rio Olympic Games. The United Nations Refugee Agency dubbed 2015, "The Year of Europe's Refugee Crisis" and Amnesty International reported that the refugee crisis was the worst in "recent history with over 19.5 million refugees across the globe" ("Global Trends".) Alongside these reports, Google Trends—which tracks and reports on the use of search terms typed into their search engine—indicates that, the popularity of the search terms "refugee" and "refugee crisis" increased in 2015 and 2016, as compared to 2013 and 2014. The linkage of "refugee" and "crisis"—a word that implies emergency and disruption—suggests the kinds of associations and meanings that were becoming attached to "refugee" during this period. The gestural mark of the butterfly helped to unsettle such potential associations and facilitated and normalized the link between Mardini—who qualified for the Olympic through unconventional channels—and other Olympic athletes who qualified for the Olympics through intense, often years-long, elite training schedules and international competitions. This signals the importance of the gestural mark of the butterfly, whose meanings subtly inflected promotional materials and their potential sets of meanings.

Inspiration in the International Order

Of course, the gestural mark was only one of the factors that shaped the meanings of Mardini's participation in the Rio Olympics, and the intersection between swimming technique, the ideology of Olympism, and the currents of power in the performance genre of sport were another important vector of her performance. The presentation of Mardini as a regular teenager in IOC-sanctioned materials intended for media circulation also helped provide an arc that supported an inspirational narrative that aligned with the principles of Olympism. Eighteen at the time of the Olympic Games, Mardini was the youngest ROT athlete, and official IOC press materials consistently emphasized the link between her age and the category of "teenager". The first line of the IOC's press release on Mardini, for instance, read "The courageous Syrian teenager is set to become the Face of the Games" ("Syrian Refugee"). Where the promotional images of the other ROT athletes predominantly show them wearing athletic gear and participating in training or sporting situations, two of the six pictures featuring Mardini capture her wearing casual clothing and smiling in non-training situations. In her autobiography, Mardini describes the photoshoots that resulted in these images. Discussing a photo in which she jumps into the air, hands above her head, feet to the side, smiling, she writes, "The teams take photos outside the stadium with the Olympic rings in the background. The IOC photographer has me jump for joy in the air. Over and over and over again" (246). This captures the intentionality of the IOC's creation of promotional materials, and while Mardini does not indicate whether other athletes were photographed for similar pictures, the image of Mardini jumping into the air is the only one of its kind in the ROT photo gallery.

The link between Mardini and conventional western conceptualizations of teenage behaviour was furthered by a short video that accompanied the press release ("Refugee Olympic Team to Shine Spotlight"). Unlike the videos for athletes such as Misenga and Anis, which list their country of origin and name only, Mardini's video begins with a placard that lists her country, name, and age. This immediately stablishes her as a teenager. Following footage of Mardini swimming, the short video features Mardini talking to the camera in front of a pool, wearing a grey hooded sweatshirt. Following this, she is shown standing in front of a stadium with the Olympic rings, wearing a track jacket and pink plaid shirt. A close-up of the back of Mardini's head prominently displays her pierced ears, adorned with several earrings on her left ear and a single silver earring on her right ear. These clothing and jewellery combinations, familiar to western audiences as the clothing of a "typical" adolescent girl, help establish Mardini as a relatable, well-adjusted teen, and the clip that follows, which shows Mardini laughing and training with teammates, furthers this association. This is important because it effectively provided the ideal bookend for Mardini's story as inflected by the ideals of Olympism. Mardini went from being a regular teenage girl who, when faced with extreme hardship, drew together courage and her athletic training to persevere, and with the eventual support of the IOC, she was able to integrate into a new teenage life in Germany and achieve her dream of competing in the Olympics.

Of course, the positive affective inflections of this narrative obscure the material realities of Mardini's experiences. In her autobiography, Mardini consistently recounts the fear and difficulty involved in leaving Syria, the challenges of her life as a refugee in Germany, and the complexities of her participation with the ROT. In relation to her experience with the ROT, specifically, she describes feeling guilty about the special privileges afforded to her as a result of her affiliation with the IOC, unease at competing at the Games without achieving the standard qualifying times, and discomfort with the media attention (241–312). She also describes the injury of repeatedly being asked to tell the boat story during press events. Relaying the experience of attending a media day, she writes:

> I look around the cluster of camera lenses. The reporters want to know what happened on the boat. I smile and tell them my story politely, but I speak without emotion. My heart closes, shuts out the vision of marching waves. Only my head is working …. I do five group interviews back to back. I say the same words, over and over again. It's impossible to relive the horror of the crossing for each reporter. My heart stays shut, I lock the calm smile onto my face. (298)

Later, she describes the cumulative effect of repeating her story to journalists: "I come to dread telling the boat story. Always the boat, often the first question. It's a mystery to me why every journalist seems excited to hear it again" (263). These quotes suggest that Mardini is aware of the complexity of her overlapping performances, and the feelings she describes experiencing are indicative of the emotional toll of the demands of the media day.

The disconnect Mardini describes between her dread and the reporters' excitement crystallizes the complex affective effects of the ideology of Olympism. The ideology of Olympism affords little room for narrative complexity. Certainly, a story can feature hardship or trauma, as Mardini's does, but to align with the principles of Olympism, difficult circumstances must serve a narrative arc that emphasizes universality, humanism, joy, and celebration. By consequence, the negative affects that might be prompted by a story of trauma are contained by structures that highlight perseverance or inspiration. For Mardini, this means that her lived experience, in both the Aegean Sea and at the press conference, are important to the media only insofar as they support this narrative, and the labour and potential harm of asking Mardini to repeatedly recount the story to reporters was not taken into consideration in her media responsibilities. Moreover, while it is impossible to know for certain why Mardini's story prompted "excitement" for the journalists, it seems likely that the story's inspirational qualities and its potential for widespread international circulation played a role in their interactions with her. Overall, then, the media day contributed to the reification of western ideologies and the logic of nation-states by asking a young stateless female of colour to participate in the packaging of her experiences for the purposes of circulating a narrative that supports the IOC's mandate.

The potential circulation of the IOC's official story was bolstered by a VISA commercial titled, "The Swim" (VISA). The commercial cross-cuts (staged) clips of Mardini racing in a pool with a re-imagining of Mardini's journey across the Aegean Sea. Over the footage, Mardini narrates, "When the engine died that night, I told myself not to give up. To give everything. I did then, and I will now". As Mardini narrates, the film cuts between images of Mardini's freestyle in the pool and a person swimming freestyle in the ocean. The commercial continues by alternating between white on black titles that read, "In 2015, Yusra Mardini helped swim her boat to safety, pulling 17 fellow refugees behind her. This August, she inspired the world to get behind her" with clips of Mardini finishing her race and smiling with the other competitors. It concludes with a voiceover by Morgan Freeman saying, "VISA is a supporter of Yusra Mardini and all refugee Olympic athletes". Building on the IOC's official narrative, the VISA commercial visually and aurally represented the rhetorical link between instances of Mardini's swimming practice and the values of Olympism. More importantly, it helped transform Mardini's story into an easily circulatable commodity that supported VISA and the IOC brand.

International Competition Without Nation: The Refugee Olympic Team

Mardini's sport performance—her enactment of the butterfly in competition at the Games—was entangled in the complex structures of international participation in the Olympics. The organizational structure of the Olympics has three main constituents: the International Olympic Committee (IOC), the ultimate authority of the Olympic movement; International Federations (IF), who administer one or several sports at the world level and encompass organizations the national level; and National Olympic Committees (NOC), who develop, promote and protect the Olympic Movement in their respective countries and send athletes to the Games ("Who We Are"). The IOC determines how many athletes participate in the Olympic Games, and, in consultation with the IFs, the number of entries for each sport. The IFs then allocate the total number of entries by region and/or nation, and the NOC's are responsible for determining how athletes or teams will be selected to fill entries. While each sport uses a different entry allocation system, swimming offers an indicative example of how the ideology of Olympism shapes the selection of athletes across Olympic sports.

In swimming, FINA allocates entries for individual events as follows: an individual who achieves an Olympic Qualifying Time, known as OQT or

"A" time, automatically qualifies for the Olympics and each nation can enter two athletes in the same event if they have both achieved the OQT. Athletes who have achieved the Olympic Standard Time, known as OST or "B" time, may also qualify for the Olympics. Following the initial qualifying period, wherein swimmers who have achieved the OQT have been selected, FINA allocates a number of additional slots and the ideology of Olympism strongly inflects this allocation stage. Based on the principles that "every individual must have the possibility of practising sport, without discrimination of any kind and in the Olympic spirit, which requires mutual understanding with a spirit of friendship, solidarity and fair play", and the mandate that the Olympics "cover all five continents" ("Olympic Charter" 13–14), FINA allocates the remaining slots based on a number of factors, including geographic and national distribution of participants (FINA 2016). As a result of this system, there are frequently considerable gaps in athletic ability between the field of participants in Olympic swimming events, and it is highly unlikely that swimmers who earned their berth in an event through a universality place will advance beyond the preliminary round.

While this system does help distribute entries to athletes from different countries, it also reveals the effects of the socio-economic and material relations that underpin elite competitive sports. The effects of this were clear in Mardini's participation in the 2016 Games. During the Olympic swim competition, Mardini swam in two races: the 100-metre freestyle and the 200-metre butterfly. Following FINA's entry allotment, she raced in the first heat of both events, competing against other athletes who earned berths in the competition through Universality Placements. In the 100-metre freestyle, she finished second to last in her heat with a time of 1:04.66. In the 100-metre butterfly, however, she won her heat with a time of 1:09.21. As was to be expected given the qualification of athletes in the first heats of Olympic swimming competitions, her time was four seconds slower than the slowest time in the second heat of the competition, eight seconds slower than the pace of the finalists, and fourteen seconds slower than the finishing time of gold-medallist Sarah Sjostrom, from Sweden, who completed the race in a time of 0:55.48. To put this in perspective, had Sjostrom and Mardini competed in the same heat, Sjostrom would have been nearly 25-metres ahead of Mardini by the end of the race. This evinces one of the underlying realities of elite, international, sports: socio-economic and material factors play a major role in shaping participation and success. In fact, sports statisticians have found that alongside size of population, a country's gross domestic product (GDP) is strongly correlated with how many medals that country will win at the Olympics (Bernard and Busse). This helps contextualize why the ROT athletes were unlikely to be top finishers in their events: it is extremely difficult for individuals without long-term infrastructures, human and material resources, financial support, or training time to excel at the Games. It also helps explain why the IOC continuously emphasized the symbolic dimensions of the ROT; from the beginning, organizers knew that the athletes were unlikely to reach the finals in their events and so framing their participation in the Games in terms of their overall placement was unlikely to produce positive stories. In Mardini's case, however, reporters, commentators, and the IOC were able to capitalize on her preliminary heat win to link athletic performance to her already widely circulated symbolic victory. The British newspaper *The Telegraph,* for instance, published an article titled "Rio 1016 Olympics: 'Incredible feeling' Syrian refugee Yusra Mardini is cheered to victory in butterfly heat" (White), while Canada's *Globe and Mail* newspaper declared that "Refugee team swimmer Yusra Mardini wins butterfly heat in symbolic victory" (Robertson).

The Many Meanings of One Athlete's Performance

The effects of Mardini's performance at the Rio Games were complex and often contradictory. On the one hand, the positive elements of Mardini's official IOC ROT narrative were not entirely inaccurate. Mardini's training as a competitive swimmer undoubtedly influenced her swim in the Aegean Sea, and the creation of the ROT also changed Mardini's life, giving her an international platform and the opportunity to compete at the Olympics. This opportunity helped facilitate further material benefits for Mardini. While the commodification of Mardini's story by brands like VISA in 2016 and Under Armour in 2017 may be opportunistic, Mardini undoubtedly received significant financial compensation for her involvement with the companies. Moreover, two years after the Rio Olympics, Mardini became the youngest ever United Nations Refugee Agency Goodwill Ambassador ("Syrian Swimmer") and published her ghost-written auto-biography *Butterfly.* The title of the book simultaneously builds on Mardini's performance of the stroke at the Olympics and capitalizes on the link between butterflies and transformation, and its contents allow Mardini to circulate her version of her story. Moreover, an email exchange that Mardini describes in the book between herself and a Syrian refugee suggests that the widespread circulation of the IOC's official narrative did offer hope or inspiration for some individuals (244).

Critically, however, the official IOC narrative regarding Mardini's performance also contributed to the reification of existing ideologies and structures of power. From their inception, the Olympic Games have restricted athlete participation based on nation-state citizenship; to compete as a French athlete meant being recognized as a subject of the nation-state of France. This not only reflected the logic of the emerging world order; it also contributed to it by staging international competitions where individual or team athletic success was explicitly linked to nation. In the early twenty-first century, the logic of nation-state citizenship undergirds the refugee crisis, as individuals who flee, reject, or are rejected by nation-states lose or are denied the rights associated with national citizenship. The ROT did draw attention to refugees and allow a few select athletes the opportunity to participate in the Games, but it did not unsettle the Olympics' participation in the reification of nation-state citizen logics, and all but ten of the 11, 238 athletes at the Rio Olympics were subject to traditional citizenship regulations and verifications. Moreover, in order to be selected for the ROT, the ten athletes had to secure official refugee status. In this context, the positive affective dimensions of Mardini's narrative supported the Olympics' continued celebration of the existing international order and functioned to obscure the more complex elements of the narrative, including the hardships of Mardini's lived experiences, the intersection between sports and socio-economics wherein any athlete without significant financial and material resources is unlikely to medal at the Games, and the western ideologies that underpin the current refugee crisis. Following the inclusion of a Refugee Olympic Team at the 2020 Summer Olympic Games, Refugee Olympic Teams appear set to become a conventional component at Summer Olympic Games. And, multiple layers of performance will likely continue to play a critical role in shaping the personal, social, and political effects of the participation of athletes who identify as refugees.

Notes

1 This is a reworked version of a previous essay, republished here with permission. Copyright (2020) "The politics of performing the butterfly stroke" From *Sporting Performances: Politics in Play* edited by Shannon Walsh authored by Kelsey Blair. Reproduced by permission of Taylor and Francis Group, LLC, a division of Informa plc.
2 This description is based on archival footage of the race. See: "Swimming Hall of Fame".
3 The historical recount of the genealogy of swimming draws from the incredibly thorough research by scholars in the last one hundred and fifty years. See: Cureton; Thomas; Colwin, *Swimming Into*; Colwin *Breakthrough*.
4 See: Colwin, *Breakthrough* 31; Doezema.

References

"Athens 1896 Swimming – Results & Videos". *International Olympic Committee*, Jan1 6, 2018, https://www.olympic.org/athens-1896/swimming.
Bernard, Andrew B. and Meghan R. Busse. "Who Wins the Olympic Games: Economic Resources and Medal Totals". *The Review of Economics and Statistics*, vol. 86, no. 1, 2004, pp. 413–17, https://doi.org/10.1162/003465304774201824.
Bourdieu, Pierre. *Distinction: A Social Critique of the Judgement of Taste*. Harvard University Press, 1984.
"Butterfly by Yusra Mardini". *Pan Macmillan*, www.panmacmillan.com/authors/yusra-mardini/butterfly/9781509881673. Accessed 1 February 2019.
"Canadian Dolphin Swim Club: Group Descriptions", *Canadian Dolphin Swim Club*, https://www.teamunify.com/SubTabGeneric.jsp?team=cancdsc&_stabid_=85647.
Colwin, Cecil. *Breakthrough Swimming*. Human Kinetics, 2002.
———. *Swimming into the 21st Century*. Leisure Press, 1992.

Cureton, Thomas Kirk. *How to Teach Swimming and Diving*. Association Press, 1934, //catalog.hathitrust.org/Record/000883937.

"Fina", *FINA.org*, http://www.fina.org/content/fina. Accessed 22 February 2019.

"Find a Program". *North Vancouver Recreation and Culture Commission*, March 28, 2016, https://www.nvrc.ca/programs-memberships/find-program/results.

Doezima, Marie. "The Murky History of the Butterfly Stroke". *The New Yorker*, Aug 11, 2018, https://www.newyorker.com/sports/sporting-scene/the-murky-history-of-the-butterfly-stroke. Accessed 22 February 2019.

Larcom, G. Clifford. "Frog, Butterfly, and Dolphin: Traditional Strokes Go the Way of the Bloomer Bathing Suits as the Engineers Revise Swimming". *Esquire*, Oct. 1936, pp. 70–80.

"Local Aquatic Empires: The Municipal Provision of Swimming Pools in England, 1828–1918". *The International Journal of the History of Sport*, vol. 24, no. 5, 2007, pp. 620–29, https://doi.org/10.1080/09523360601183160.

"London 1908 Summer Olympics – Results & Video Highlights", *Olympic*, https://www.olympic.org/london-1908. Accessed 22 February 2019.

Love, Christopher. "An Overview of the Development of Swimming in England, c.1750–1918". *The International Journal of the History of Sport*, vol. 24, no. 5, May 2007, pp. 568–85. Taylor and Francis+NEJM, doi:10.1080/09523360601183095.44.

———. "Local Aquatic Empires: The Municipal Provision of Swimming Pools in England, 1828–1918". *The International Journal of the History of Sport*, vol. 24, no. 5, 2007, pp. 620–29, doi:10.1080/09523360601183160.

"Melbourne/Stockholm 1956 Swimming – Results & Videos". *Olympic*, Nov 19, 2017, https://www.olympic.org/melbourne-/-stockholm-1956/swimming.

Millon, Drew. "Syrian Refugee Swimmer Yusra Mardini Wins First Heat of 100M Butterfly but Doesn't Qualify for Semifinals at Rio Olympics". *ABC News*, https://abcnews.go.com/International/syrian-refugee-swimmer-yusra-mardini-wins-heat-100m/story?id=41169590. Accessed 9 February 2019.

Noland, Carrie. *Agency and Embodiment: Performing Gestures/Producing Culture*. Harvard University Press, 2009.

"Olympic Charter – Downloads All the Charters from 1908–2016". *Olympic*, July 12, 2019, https://www.olympic.org/olympic-studies-centre/collections/official-publications/olympic-charters.

"Olympic Charter & Other Official IOC Documents | Downloads", *Olympic*, July 31, 2019, https://www.olympic.org/documents/olympic-charter.

"Rio 2016: Inspirational Refugee Mardini Revels in Swimming Victory". *Yahoo Sports*, http://sports.yahoo.com/news/rio-2016-inspirational-refugee-mardini-222033041.html. Accessed 9 February 2019.

Orme, Nicholas and Christopher Middleton. *Early British Swimming, 55 BC–AD 1719: With the First Swimming Treatise in English, 1595*. University of Exeter, 1983.

———. *Early British Swimming, 55 BC–AD 1719: With the First Swimming Treatise in English, 1595*. University of Exeter, 1983.

"Refugee Olympic Team". *Olympic*, Dec 20, 2018, https://www.olympic.org/refugee-olympic-team.

"Refugee Olympic Team to Shine Spotlight on Worldwide Refugee Crisis". *Olympic*, Jan 25, 2017, https://www.olympic.org/news/refugee-olympic-team-to-shine-spotlight-on-worldwide-refugee-crisis.

"Refugee Olympic Team to Shine Spotlight on Worldwide Refugee Crisis – Olympic News", *Olympic,* https://www.olympic.org/news/refugee-olympic-team-to-shine-spotlight-on-worldwide-refugee-crisis. Accessed 1 February 2019.

"Representing Refugees: Yusra Mardini". *Olympic,* December 20, 2018, https://www.olympic.org/news/representing-refugees-yusra-mardini.

"Rio 2016". *Olympic,* https://www.olympic.org/rio-2016. Accessed 28 January 2019.

"Rio 2016 200m Butterfly Women – Olympic Swimming", *Olympic,* https://www.olympic.org/rio-2016/swimming/200m-butterfly-women.

"Rio 2016 Sets Records on the Field of Play and Online", Olympic, https://www.olympic.org/news/rio-2016-sets-records-on-the-field-of-play-and-online-1.

Robertson, Grant. "Refugee Team Swimmer Yusra Mardini Wins Butterfly Heat in Symbolic Victory – The Globe and Mail". *The Globe and Mail,* 6 August 2016, https://www.theglobeandmail.com/sports/olympics/refugee-team-swimmer-yusra-mardini-wins-butterfly-heat-in-symbolic-victory/article31302129/.

Roche, Maurice. *Megaevents and Modernity: Olympics and Expos in the Growth of Global Culture.* Routledge, 2002. www-taylorfrancis-com.ezproxy.library.ubc.ca, doi:10.4324/9780203443941.

Sinclair, Archibald and William Henry. *Swimming.* Longmans, Green, and Company, 1893.

Southgate, Martha. "Water Damage: More Blacks Lack Swimming Skills – The New York Times". *The New York Times,* 10 August 2012, https://www.nytimes.com/2012/08/11/opinion/water-damage-more-blacks-lack-swimming-skills.html.

Swimming Hall of Fame. "1936 Olympic 200 Breaststroke – YouTube". *YouTube,* March 2012, https://www.youtube.com/watch?v=l-R4wiSZcRc.

"Swimming Lessons – Canadian Red Cross". *Red Cross Canada,* http://www.redcross.ca/training-and-certification/course-descriptions/swimming-and-water-safety-courses/swimming-lessons. Accessed 23 February 2019.

"Syrian Refugee MARDINI (ROT) Swims for Joy after Swimming for Her Life", *Olympic,* Jan. 2017, https://www.olympic.org/news/syrian-refugee-mardini-rot-swims-for-joy-after-swimming-for-her-life.

"Syrian Swimmer Yusra Mardini Appointed UNHCR Goodwill Ambassador". *United Nations,* April 28, 2017, https://www.un.org/youthenvoy/2017/04/syrian-swimmer-yusra-mardini-appointed-unhcr-goodwill-ambassador/.

"Team of Refugee Olympic Athletes (ROA) Created by the IOC – Olympic News". *Olympic,* Jan 25 2017, https://www.olympic.org/news/team-of-refugee-olympic-athletes-roa-created-by-the-ioc.

"The Inspirational Olympic Journey of Refugee Swimmer Yusra Mardini – Olympic News". *Olympic,* Apr. 2017, https://www.olympic.org/news/the-inspirational-olympic-journey-of-refugee-swimmer-yusra-mardini.

"The Refugee Olympic Team, a Symbol of Hope – Olympic News". *Olympic,* May 5, 2017, https://www.olympic.org/news/the-refugee-olympic-team-a-symbol-of-hope.

"The Rise of the 'Dolphin Kick' | Seoul 1988". *Olympic Channel,* https://www.olympicchannel.com/en/video/detail/the-rise-of-the-dolphin-kick-seoul-1988/. Accessed 23 February 2019.

"Global Trends Forced Displacement", *United Nations Humans Rights Council* https://www.unhcr.org/flagship-reports/globaltrends/globaltrends2019/

"Figures at a Glance". *UNHCR*, https://www.unhcr.org/figures-at-a-glance.html. Accessed 4 March 2019.

Thomas, Ralph. *Swimming*. Sampson Low, Martson & Company, 1904.

"Who We Are". *International Olympic Committee*, January 31, 2019, https://www.olympic.org/about-ioc-olympic-movement?sc_site=website&.

Winterton, Rachel. "'A Question of Propriety?' Women's Competitive Swimming in Melbourne, 1893–1900". *The International Journal of the History of Sport*, vol. 26, no. 14, 2009, pp. 2086–105, https://doi.org/10.1080/09523360903303052.

Wasserrettungswesen, ARGE Österreichisches. *ARGE*. February 23, 2019, http://www.schwimmabzeichen.at/de/arge.

VISA Europe. "Visa | The Swim – YouTube". *YouTube*, https://www.youtube.com/watch?v=7EytXrPcSTM. Accessed 1 February 2019.

CONCLUSION

Peruvian soccer fans bombard the field during a 1964 match against Argentina. The riot that follows the bombardment kills 300 people and is widely considered the worst soccer-related riot of the late twentieth century.

Kathrine Switzer holds her balance while being pushed by male competitors during the 1967 Boston Marathon. She fends off her attacker and completes the race, becoming the first woman to officially complete the Boston marathon.

Lee Jae-Woon and Kim Hyun Mee light the Paralympic Flame during the 1988 Paralympic Opening Ceremonies in Seoul. It is the first time the Olympic flame is included in a Paralympic Games.

In the crowded stands of a European football in 2012, two presidents—Serge Sarkisan of Armenia and Abdullah Gul of Turkey—stand beside one another. With the border between the two countries having been closed since the early 1990s, the meeting marks the first time a Turkish leader visits Armenia in 21 years.

On a hot August day in 2016, the playing of the American national anthem prompts young man and football player Colin Kaepernick to kneel on the sidelines of a football field. His gesture—a protest against racial injustice, police brutality, and systemic oppression in the United States—sparks nationwide debate and inspires similar protests in a range of professional and amateur sporting contexts.

From the bodily harm that resulted from the 1964 Estadio Nacional disaster in Peru to Switzer's individual and symbolic achievement to the increasing acknowledgement of the capacities of disabled bodies-minds signalled by the lighting of the Paralympic flame to a tentative geo-political relationship between Armenia and Turkey to the social activism of Colin Kaepernick's kneel, each of the above scenes had effects that rippled across individual, social, cultural, and political domains. While actions that take place in connection to high-profile sport performances may be exceptional in scope, their dense web of connections and effects are not unusual. As the case study in the previous chapter suggests, extraordinary sport performances emerge from and contribute to already existing ecologies of practices, activities, and events. Long before Yusra Mardini swam in the Aegean Sea or the Olympic Games, she learned the technique of the freestyle and butterfly strokes, the latter of which emerged from the experimentation of competitive swimmers in the 1930s, connecting Mardini to an extended genealogy of practice and to the area of technique of swimming more broadly. Such wafting and weaving connections suggest how the tendrils of sport performance extend beyond the boundaries of a single genre or socio-cultural domain and further demonstrate why we might study sport through the lens of performance. Four snapshot case studies suggest the generative potential of exploring such links.

Snapshot 1: The Vertical Plane and the Patterning of Behaviours Across Practices and Activities

As I outlined in the first chapter, the principle of verticality plays a key role in the patterning of skills in basketball. In fact, verticality is important in a range of areas of specialized practice from rhythmic gymnastics—where vertical and horizontal axes are used in evaluation and scoring—to surfing—where "going vertical" refers to a move where the surfer's board is on top of the wave while the surfer is to the side of the board—to vertical dance—wherein dancers use harnesses and ropes to dance on walls. In some cases, the role of verticality may have little resonance with the behaviours of basketball. In other instances, however, there may be meaningful connections between areas of technique and practice. Ballet offers an indicative, and perhaps unexpected, example. Originating in Italian courts in the fifteenth century and developing in French courts in the sixteenth and seventeen centuries, the technique of ballet was initially a participatory dance performed by noble persons, including members of the monarchy.[1] During this early period, the principle of verticality as articulated through vertical carriage, wherein an erect, upright, posture was associated with nobility and esteem. Over time, ballet moved from the realm of participatory dance to theatrical dance, and as a result of several factors—including the codification of ballet in French academies in the seventeenth century and the development of the point shoe and its accompanying technique—the principle of verticality solidified as a central element of ballet practice. As Sandra Noll Hammond writes, "Even more fundamental to ballet technique than the five positions of the feet was and is the vertical, balanced stance of the dancer" ("The rise of Ballet Technique" 70).

To enact the verticality that is so central to ballet practice, dancers need to develop muscular strength and control in their toes, feet, ankles, calves, hips, and abdomen in order to perform and display verticality. They also need to acquire the ability to recognize and internalize the significance of the vertical plane in ballet and to believe in their own capacity to perform in accordance with this principle. This echoes the embodied learning of basketball, where players must learn to pattern their movements in accordance with the principle of the vertical plane, ensuring that they do not cross the horizontal axis and crash into the space of other players, which requires the development of physical and mental aptitudes. The specific function of verticality in basketball and ballet obviously differs; in ballet, verticality patterns both individual and interpersonal movements whereas in basketball verticality predominantly pertains to interpersonal movements. Nevertheless, verticality offers a connective thread between the two seemingly disparate practices, and these resonances suggest potential routes for further investigation.

Snapshot 2: Sport Spectacles and Their Stadiums, the Infrastructural Effects of Sport Events

Extending out from practice to occasions, studying sport can also illuminate cross-domain and cross-disciplinary connections. Every day of the week in urban centres around the world, hundreds, and often thousands, of people are drawn to public venues to move in and be moved by regularly scheduled, secular spectacle performances such as such as Cirque du Soleil-style "nouveau cirque" shows, professional sporting contests such as football, hockey, or cricket matches, and arena-housed musical performances. These spectacles play a critical role in shaping everyday urban lives: their architectural and infrastructural demands influence civic policy and planning; their large gatherings draw people into concentrated areas, affecting a city's temporal rhythms and geographical flows; and their occasions offer opportunities for individuals to interact with each other and develop their civic identities. Though the performance genres of such spectacles are distinct, their configurations share key overlaps. Namely, the size of the gatherings, and the technical requirements of the shows, require special venues. Sporting arenas are often used for these spectacles. For example, in Montreal, Canada—the city where I currently live—the city's major multipurpose arena, Centre Bell, is owned and operated by the group that owns NHL hockey team the Montreal Canadiens. Hockey is not the only performing occasion to take place within the arena, however. As with akin civic stadiums in metropolis throughout Canada and the United States such as Rogers Arena in Vancouver, British Columbia or Crypto Arena in Los Angeles, Centre Bell is the city's main venue for spectacle-scale touring concerts, theatre shows, circus production, and other major entertainment events. While such multidisciplinary hosting capacities are integrated into the building's design and architecture, the stadium is first and foremost the Canadiens' home arena, and traces of sport are everywhere, from the hydraulic jumbo screen above the middle of the rink to the interior wall decorations—which feature celebrations of the team's history—to the renaming of the street where the stadium situated. To this final item, on the 100th anniversary of the Montreal Canadiens, a section of Rue de la Gauchetiere Ouest was renamed Avenue des Canadiens-de-Montreal in honour of the Canadiens and their home stadium ("Inauguration"). As such, performances that are *not* Montreal Canadiens' games are essentially guests in the sporting space. This has a range of implications for the performances that take place in this space from issues relating to scheduling, spatial arrangements (and their implications for blocking and choreography), sound amplification, and lighting as well as the impact for audience members including sightlines, acoustics, and ambience. And, while the details of Centre Bell are specific to the Canadiens and Montreal, the arena is indicative of the cross-disciplinary use of arena-style stadiums around the world, including Madison Square Garden in New York, Wembley Stadium in London, Cairo Stadium in Cairo, and Beijing National Stadium in Beijing, all of which are sport facilities that also host multidisciplinary events.

Snapshot 3: Sport and Video Games— Connections between Genres

Alongside practices and occasions, studying sport through the lens of performance facilitates cross-disciplinary analysis of genres and forms. In this regard, it is certainly possible to put sport in conversation with established performance genres such as theatre and dance, but it is also possible to examine the relationship between sport and emergent genres such as video games. Sport-based video games offer users the opportunity to play as coaches, players, or managers. Games range from basic games with simple graphics—where users direct pucks into nets, for example—to complex games with high resolution, filmic-quality, graphics and complicated gameplay, where users complete multiple simultaneous tasks. Such games represent sporting practices and action and also borrow elements from the configurations of sport, including rules and the segmentation of time. In addition to representation of sporting action, branches of video game and sport also share the form of contest. To this end, esports do not (necessarily) involve sporting action; rather, *esport* refers to organized video game competitions. These competitions use tournament formats where players, who might compete individually or in teams, play against one another in several rounds of play. In the twenty-first century, such competitions have become progressively professionalized, and there are international leagues and circuits where players can earn hundreds of thousands of dollars in prizes. In addition to the obvious overlaps in nomenclature, sports organizations such as the International Olympic Committee have recognized esports as a potentially emergent genre of sport (Biesler) The similarities and distinctions between video games and established sports open up key questions for performance researchers. What are the similarities between the areas of technique of video games, which tend to involve fine motor skills, and the areas of technique of sports, which tend to involve gross motor skills? What are the embodied, epistemological, and ideological effects of combining the configurational aspects of sports—organization, competition, etc.—with the representational facets of video games, which sometimes depict scenarios of violence? Future studies of sport and performance can begin to formulate responses to such lines of inquiry.

Snapshot 4: Points of Disjuncture—In Politics Differences Between Genres Matters

Investigating sport also helps identify meaningful points of disjuncture between performances and domains. From identifying "front runners" (leaders) of campaigns to "hail mary" (desperate, unlikely to succeed) efforts to pass legislature, the realm of politics has long been rife with sports metaphors and analogies. When it comes to leadership debates, the language of boxing is particularly popular. In Canada in 2015, for example, newspaper *The Ottawa Sun* published an article that tracked "The Five Knockout Moments in Political Debates in Canada" and a year later, in the United States 2016, an *L.A. Times* headline, commenting on the presidential debate between candidates Hillary Clinton and Donald Trump, noted that "[r]ound by round our analysts say Clinton out punched Trump". And, frequently, much of the media discourse that follows debates attempts to identify the so-called winners and losers. Political debates do have important overlaps with sport. In competitive debate—which is part of the performance genre of sport—teams of participants compete against one another and are judged based on a list of criteria. The located configurations of competitive debate vary, but competitive debating usually involves clear rules and action is usually sequences so that multiple speakers perform in successive rounds (first speaker, second speaker, etc.). Political debates, too, frequently involve competition, pre-determined rules, and rounds. Critically, however, political debates do not involve formal judges nor do they feature an official ranking of participants. This creates a key disjuncture between political and sporting debate. Unlike competitive debaters, whose performances are judged by field experts and ranked based on pre-determined criteria, politicians are evaluated by individuals within a general audience, and there are no set factors that determine assessment. As such, there are no *actual* winners or losers of political debate, and the main indicator of a debate's victor is determined by the debates impact on campaign momentum and later votes. In a political debate, then, a candidate can appear to "lose" the debate in terms of content, style, and strategy (three criteria frequently used in competitive debate) but ultimately "win" the debate based on other factors such as personality or general appeal. Arguably, this is what happened in the 2016 American election, wherein Democratic candidate Hillary Clinton appeared stronger in relation to conventional debate criteria but ultimately lost the election to Republican candidate Donald Trump. This is not to say that commentators should refrain from using sport metaphors. Rather, it signals the limits of comparison, which provides an essential parameter for cross-genre analysis.

The Next Game

The snapshot case studies suggest the range of links between sport and other domains of performance and culture. But there is still much work to do both within sport and between sport and other genres and domains. To these ends, while I have attempted to account for a range of relations and intersections, the complexity of the matrix of circuits in the performance genre of sport has meant that I have left some areas under-examined. Future research in the field of the intersections between sport and consumerism, sport and ability, sport and illness/injury, or sport and sexuality (amongst other topics) is needed. Moreover, I have gestured toward the possibility of cross-disciplinary analysis, but in the interest of clarity have sometimes omitted (or cut) in-depth discussion of other genres. Such work is critical for the continued development of the study of sport in the field of performance and for the field more broadly.

Even more pressing than the development of the field is the rigorous understandings of sporting practices, activities, and events. The 2016 American presidential debate offers one instance where sporting language was used to communicate across domains. Politics is not the only realm where sports metaphors abound. From business to current events, sport metaphors can be a way of framing and understanding the world. But sports are not only an entry point for understanding and communicating about the happenings of contemporary life. As the case studies in this book begin to demonstrate, sport performances can make worlds—personal, cultural, social, and sometimes even political. The disqualification of eight women's badminton players from an Olympic Games in 2012 had profound personal effects for the players—who were denied the opportunity to continue to compete in one of the world's most prestigious sporting festivals after years of training. The principles underpinning the vertical plane principle might have personal, philosophical, and pedagogical effects for basketball performance. Audience behaviours may change and evolve, but the enactments of Canadian hockey spectators are connected to one another across time, continuously shaping hockey's position in Canada's national imaginary and the texture of Canadian conceptions of nation. The logics of gridiron football shape the bodily, social, and cultural impacts of injury mini-dramas in the United States. These cases signal the intimate bond between sport performances and their socio-political contexts, wherein sport performances are both shaped by and continuously shaping the conditions in which they are enacted. Continued attention to such performances is, therefore, crucial for the development of nuanced and novel understandings of both sport and performance in the twenty-first century.

Note

1 For more on the history of ballet, see: Astier; Kant; Hammond "Steps through Time."

References

Astier, Regine. "Academie Royale De Danse", *International Encyclopedia of Dance*, Oxford Press, 1998.

Bay, Julianne, "The Five Knockout Moments in Political Debates in Canada", *Ottawa Sun*, August 5, 2015, https://ottawasun.com/2015/08/05/the-top-5-knockout-moments-in-political-debates-in-canada

Biseler, Des, "IOC Announces Inaugural Slate of Olympic-Licensed Esports Events," *The Washington Post,* April 22, 2021, https://www.washingtonpost.com/video-games/esports/2021/04/22/ioc-olympics-esports/

Hamond, Sandra Noll. "The Rise of Ballet Technique and Training: The Professionalisation of an Art Form," in *The Cambridge Companion to Ballet*, edited by Marion Kant, Cambridge University Press, 2007, p. 70, https://doi.org/10.1017/CCOL9780521832212.008.

———. "Steps through Time: Selected Dance Vocabulary of the Eighteenth and Nineteenth Centuries." *Dance Research: The Journal of the Society for Dance Research*, vol. 10, no. 2, 1992, pp. 93–108.

"Inauguration of avenue des Canadiens-de-Montréal," NHL, October 9, 2009, https://www.nhl.com/canadiens/news/inauguration-of-avenue-des-canadiens-de-montreal/c-501614

Kant, Marion. *The Cambridge Companion to Ballet*. Cambridge University Press, 2011.

"Round by round our analysts say Clinton out punched Trump," *L.A. Times,* September 26, 2016, https://www.latimes.com/projects/la-na-pol-first-debate-scorecard/

APPENDIX 1

LIST OF SPORTS SURVEYED

3-on-3 Basketball	*Football*	*Ski Jumping*
Aikido	Football 5-a-side	Snowboarding
Alpine Skiing	Freestyle Wrestling	Softball
Archery	Freestyle Skiing	Speed Skating
Artistic Gymnastics	Goal Ball	Sport Climbing
Athletics	Golf	Surfing
Badminton	Greco-Roman Wrestling	Swimming
Baseball	Handball	Synchronized Swimming
Basketball	Ice Hockey	Table Tennis
Basque Pelota	Judo	Taekwondo
Biathlon	Karate	Tennis
BMX Freestyle	Lacrosse	Track Cycling
BMX Racing	Luge	Trampoline
Bobsleigh	Marathon Swimming	Triathlon
Boccia	Modern Pentathlon	Tug of War
Bowling	Mountain Biking	Volleyball (Beach)
Boxing	Nordic Combined	Volleyball (Indoor)
Canoe/Kayak (Slalom)	Para Athletics	Water Motorsport
Canoe/Kayak (Sprint)	Para Dance Sport	Water Polo
Cheerleading	Polo	Weightlifting
Cricket	Powerlifting	Wheelchair Basketball
Croquet	Rackets	Wheelchair Fencing
Cross Country Skiing	Rhythmic Gymnastics	Wheelchair Rugby
Curling	Road Cycling	Wheelchair Tennis
Darts	Roque	Wushu
Diving	Rowing	
Equestrian (Dressage)	Rugby	
Equestrian (Vaulting)	Rugby Sevens	

3-on-3 Basketball	*Football*	*Ski Jumping*
Equestrian (Eventing)	Sailing	
Equestrian (Jumping)	Shooting	
Fencing	Short Track Speed Skating	
Field Hockey	Skateboarding	
Figure Skating	Skeleton	

INDEX

activity: and configuration 45, 50, 56–58, 60–61, 68, 74, 80, 91–93, 111–114; and basketball 25, 27, 29–31; and hockey 67–71, 74; theory of 7, 13, 23, 61–67, 90, 99
affect 48–49, 72–73, 98
assemblage 21–23, 38
audience: and affect 72–74, 99, 101; and behaviour 101, 105; configuration 67–71, 73, 93–94; and formation 70, 74–75; and liveness 75–59; and orientation 69–70, 73, 77–79; and performance studies 65–57; and performance event 65–57, 90–92; and practice 70–72; and twentieth century Canadian hockey 72–29; and twenty-first century Canadian hockey 79–85

badminton 11–13, 18–19, 24, 30, 32, 34, 36, 38, 135
ballet 7, 29, 56, 131–132
basketball: in Canada 43–44, 50–55, 56–6; and configuration (general) 45–50; and configuration (located) 50–55; and formation 56–61, 132; history of 43–44, 46–47, 50–55, 59–60; and women 50–55, 58, 59–61
butterfly 14, 110–111, 113–116, 119–120, 124–125

dance: and configuration 45, 47; performance of 2–3; as performance genre 6, 8–11, 20, 22, 28, 67, 77; as technique 56, 9– 92; and ballet 131
drama: 71, 73, 78, 82, 98–99; *see also* mini-drama

event *see* performance event

female athlete 36–38, 54
football: association 44, 56, 95; and configuration 91, 101, 102; history of gridiron 95–98; and mini-drama 102–106, National Football League (NFL) 98–106
formation: *see also* basketball; and patterning of audience behaviour 68–69, 72–75, 79–81, 92, 94; and patterning of performer behaviour 9, 12–13, 42–44, 51, 57–61, 112–113
frame 44, 57

gender: and identity 6, 8, 11; and match fixing 19, 26, 36–38; and power 26; and performativity 6, 115; sex and verification policies 36–38; and women 61, 11

hockey: *see also* audience; game of 11, 13, 28–29, 33, 59, 101, 132; history in Canada 72–85

International Olympic Committee: and badminton 36–38; and genre 14, 32–33; and hockey 65, 81, 83; and swimming 111–112, 116–121, 123, 123, 125–126

liveness 76–77

media 35, 76–77, 83–84, 110–111, 117–118, 122, 134; and social media 81–82
mini-drama 13, 91–92, 98, 103–104

Noland, C. 10, 115

occasion 6–7, 19, 65–66, 81, 94, 99
Olympic Games 11, 13–14, 18, 20, 25–26, 32
orientation 44, 47–48, 54, 68–70, 72–73, 77–79

performance event: theory of 6, 13, 27, 57, 65–67, 90–94; and hockey 74, 76
performance genre: sport as 22–30, 38, 91, 111–112, 114, 116, 134–135; and spectacle 79–80; theory of 3–4, 6, 9, 12–13, 18–22, 79, 91, 131
performance studies: field of 1–9, 12–13, 19–20, 27, 46, 91; scholars 10, 20, 44, 55, 76
practice: and audience 65–67, 70, 72–74, 79, 91–92; *see also* basketball; as common occurrence 36, 38, 118; and configuration 43, 56–61, 91–91, 112–113; and football 99, 101–102; and performance genre 23, 26–28, 31–32; *see also* swimming; theory of 5, 5–9, 11–13; and the vertical plane 131–132

ritual 3, 9, 19–20, 27, 44

Schechner, R. 6, 8–9, 20, 27, 44, 55
Spatz, B. 7, 56, 67
spectacle 79
sport: *see* performance genre
swimming: and activity configuration 119–126; and the butterfly stroke 14, 110–117; practice of 4, 11–12, 21, 29, 38, 45, 56–57, 68, 92, 131

Taylor, D. 6, 8, 10–11, 44, 55
technique: and audience behaviours 70, 72, 75, 80; and participants 91, 102, 111; and sport as a performance genre 9–10, 21, 23–24, 27–28; and swimming 113–116, 120,134; theory of 5, 7, 21, 56–60, 131
theatre: as genre 77, 80, 92, 103; as performance event 44–46, 47, 56–57, 132–133; and performance studies 3, 6, 8–9, 18–20, 27; and western repertory theatre 29, 66–67

vertical plane 13, 51–55, 61, 132
verticality 131–132

For Product Safety Concerns and Information please contact our EU representative GPSR@taylorandfrancis.com
Taylor & Francis Verlag GmbH, Kaufingerstraße 24, 80331 München, Germany

www.ingramcontent.com/pod-product-compliance
Lightning Source LLC
Chambersburg PA
CBHW051403290426
44108CB00015B/2131